CW00684123

NEW MILLS TO SHEFFIELD

and Hayfield

Vic Mitchell & Keith Smith

MP Middleton Press

Front cover: This gives a good impression of the Peak District, through which much of the route passes. The coal train is emerging from Cowburn Tunnel and it is approaching Edale station, which is the closest one to the Peak itself. Class 45 no. D108 is seen on 6th May 1966. (Colour-Rail.com)

Back cover: Railway Clearing House map from 1947.

Published April 2020

ISBN 978 1 910356 44 9

Cover design Deborah Esher
Design Cassandra Morgan

Published by
> *Middleton Press*
> *Easebourne Lane*
> *Midhurst*
> *West Sussex*
> *GU29 9AZ*
Tel: 01730 813169
Email: info@middletonpress.co.uk
www.middletonpress.co.uk

Printed and bound by CPI Group (UK) Ltd, Croydon, CR0 4YY

INDEX

65	Bamford	10	Hayfield
97	Beauchief	17	Hazel Grove (Midland)
8	Birch Vale	105	Heeley
19	Buxworth	57	Hope (Derbyshire)
23	Chinley	1	New Mills Central
89	Dore & Totley	99	Millhouses & Ecclesall
39	Edale	112	Sheffield
79	Grindleford	107	Sheffield Midland
73	Hathersage		

ACKNOWLEDGEMENTS

We are very grateful for the assistance received from many of those mentioned in the credits, also from C.Booth, A.J.Castledine, G.Croughton, G.Gartside, C.M.Howard, N.Langridge, B.Lewis, D. and Dr S. Salter, T.Walsh, and in particular our always supportive families.

I. Our route is shown with a dark line on this Railway Clearing House map from 1947.

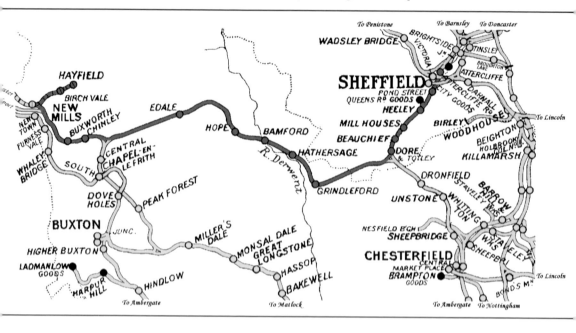

GEOGRAPHICAL SETTING

Coal deposits are beyond both the east and west ends of our route, which is mostly across the High Peak District. This raised area is composed mainly of limestones that contain some volcanic ash and thin layers of lead, once extensively worked. The lime from limestone aided the production of mortar, whitewash, paper and, eventually, cement. This domed district has required extensive tunnels and is the source of many rivers. Only one early line passed over its surface and it is featured in our volume called *Cromford & High Peak*.

Rivers on the east side include the Noe and notably the Ashop and Derwent. These two feed the three massive reservoirs north of Bamford. On the west side, the Hayfield branch was in the valley of the River Sett, while our route from New Mills to Chinley follows, first, the River Goyt and then the Black Brook. On this were three mills.

The opportunities for mineral working and tourism appear in the photographs which follow. They were mostly taken in Derbyshire. The boundary with the West Riding of Yorkshire was just south of Dore.

The maps are to the scale of 25ins to 1 mile, with north at the top, unless otherwise indicated.

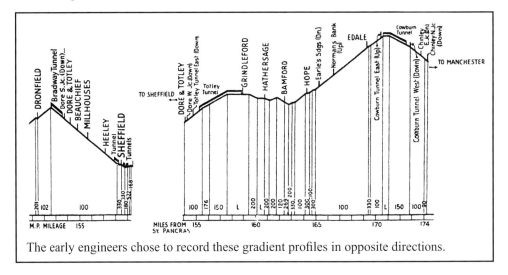

The early engineers chose to record these gradient profiles in opposite directions.

HISTORICAL BACKGROUND

The Sheffield & Rotherham Railway, a constituent of the Midland Railway, opened on 1st November 1838. It was met from the south by the Midland's direct line from Chesterfield to Sheffield on 1st February 1870, when the new (and current) Sheffield station was opened.

New Mills saw its first trains in 1857, when the Stockport, Disley & Whaley Bridge Railway arrived. The second station at New Mills, later New Mills Central, opened on 1st July 1865 on the line from Marple. On 1st March 1868, this was extended to Hayfield and appears herein. These lines were built by the Manchester Sheffield & Lincolnshire Railway and were operated by the Sheffield & Midland Committee from 1869 and the Great Central Railway & Midland Committee from 1904.

The route south from New Mills to Millers Dale was opened in 1866 by the MR and it joined its 1863 line between Buxton and Hassop at Peak Forest Junction.

The Dore & Chinley Railway was opened for goods on 11th June 1893 and its passenger stations were opened on 13th May 1894, by the MR.

On 1st July 1901, the Midland opened a direct line from New Mills South Junction to Cheadle. It enabled the MR to run its expresses to Manchester Central instead of London Road.

Upon the grouping of 1923, the MR became part of the London Midland & Scottish Railway. With the advent of nationalisation on 1st January 1948, this formed mainly the London Midland Region of BR. Boundary changes on 2nd April 1950 moved some lines to the Eastern Region. The Hayfield branch was closed on 5th January 1970. Freight closures are shown in the captions.

Under privatisation, services west of Dore were provided by three operators. Regional Railways North East operated from 2nd March 1997 and was re-branded as Northern Spirit in May 1998. This became Arriva Trains Northern from 27th April 2001. Also operating on the route from 2nd March 1997 was North Western Trains, which was re-branded to First North Western in 1998. As part of a remapping of services in the north of England, two new franchises were designed and let. A new TransPennine Express franchise was created on 1st February 2004, operated by First-Keolis. This was replaced by another TransPennine Express franchise on 1st April 2016, run by First. A new Northern franchise was also created on 12th December 2004, operated by Serco-Abellio. This was replaced by another new Northern franchise on 1st April 2016, run by Arriva. Also, Central Trains (operated by National Express) ran between 2nd March 1997 and 10th November 2007.

North of Dore, Midland Mainline (also operated by National Express) ran from 28th April 1996 until 10th November 2007, while Virgin Cross Country operated between 6th January 1997 and 10th November 2007. All services (from west and south) ran north of Dore to Sheffield. Central Trains and Midland Mainline services became part of East Midlands Trains (operated by Stagecoach) from 11th November 2007, while Virgin Cross Country services transferred to CrossCountry (operated by Arriva) on the same day.

The EMT franchise ended on 17th August 2019 and was replaced by East Midlands Railway. The Northern franchise ended early, on 1st March 2020, and was thereafter operated directly by the Department for Transport.

PASSENGER SERVICES

Trains arriving at New Mills in November 1865 from Manchester and Marple numbered eight on weekdays and three on Sundays. The extension south to Peak Forest and beyond in 1867 brought a frequency of four and two. The Hayfield branch received eight and three by 1869, all starting in Manchester.

The number of trains stopping at most stations on the Hope Valley line between Hope and Sheffield are shown below:

	Weekdays	Sundays
1894	5	3
1924	10	5
1948	13	6
1969	9	6
2001	11	12

The New Mills to Hayfield service examples were thus:

	Weekdays	Sundays
1894	13	4
1924	13	4
1948	15	8
1968	21	15

June 1869

MANCHESTER, HYDE, MARPLE, NEW MILLS, and HAYFIELD.—M., S., and L.

Mls	Fares. 1 cl.	2 cl.	3 cl.																	Sundays.				
				M'chestr (Lon. Rd.)	7 30	10 5	1130	1240	1 15	1 50	2 25	4 30	5 5	6 10	7 15	8 35	9 30	1050	....	7 50	1 55	3 30	6 15	9 0
¾				Ardwick ....[Vue	7 34	10 9	1134	1243	1 19	1 53	2 29	4 33	5 8	6 13	7 19	8 38	9 34	10 5	....	7 54	1 58	3 34	6 19	9 4
1½	0 6	0 3	0 1½	Ashbury's, for Belle	7 37	1012	1135	1246	1 22	....	....	....	....	....	7 22	....	9 37	10 8	....	7 57	2 1	....	6 22	9 7
2½	0 6	0 4	0 2½	Gorton	7 40	1015	1142	1249	1 25	....	2 35	....	....	....	7 26	....	9 40	1012	....	8 0	2 4	3 41	6 25	9 10
3½	0 6	0 4	0 3	Fairfield	7 44	1019	1146	1253	1 29	....	2 39	4 39	....	....	7 30	....	9 44	1016	....	8 4	2 8	3 45	6 29	9 14
5	0 11	0 8½	0 5	Guide Bridge	7 50	1025	1153	1259	1 35	2 11	2 46	4 45	5 17	6 22	7 36	8 51	9 50	1030	....	8 10	2 14	3 53	6 35	9 25
6½	1 1	0 10	0 6	Hyde Junction	7 54	1029	....	1 2	....	2 15	2 50	4 48	....	TuF	7 40	....	....	1034	....	8 16	2 18	3 57	6 39	9 30
7	1 2	0 11	0 7	Hyde	7 57	1032	12 1	1 5	1 41	2 18	2 54	4 51	5 23	6 27	7 43	8 56	9 56	1037	....	8 20	2 21	4 0	6 43	9 34
8½	1 8	1 3	0 8½	Woodley Junc.*	8 2	1038	12 6	1 9	1 46	2 23	3 0	4 55	5 28	6 32	7 48	9 1	10 1	1042	....	8 26	2 26	4 4	6 48	9 39
10	1 11	1 5	0 10	Romiley	8 6	1042	....	....	1 50	....	3 4	....	5 32	6 36	7 52	....	10 4	Sats. only.	....	8 31	2 30	....	6 52	....
11½	2 0	1 6	0 11½	Marple	8 11	1046	....	....	1 55	....	3 9	....	5 36	6 40	7 57	....	10 8		....	8 36	2 35	....	6 57	....
13½	2 4	1 8	1 1½	Strines	8 15	1050	....	....	1 59	....	F.S.	....	5 40	....	8 1	....	1012		....	8 41	2 39	....	7 1	....
15½	2 6	1 8	1 1½	New Mills	8 20	1055	....	....	2 3	....	3 17	....	5 45	6 48	8 5	....	1016		....	8 45	2 43	....	7 5	....
17½	2 10	1 11	1 3	Birch Vale	8 25	F.S.	....	....	2 8	....	Sat.	....	5 50	Sat.	8 10	....	Sat.		....	8 50	2 48	....	7 10	....
18½	3 1	2 1	1 4½	Hayfield ....arr	8 30	11 5	....	....	2 13	....	3 23	....	5 55	6 56	8 15	....	1025		....	8 55	2 58	....	7 15	....

MANCHESTER, BUXTON, CHINLEY, HOPE, SHEFFIELD, and THE NORTH.—Midland.

Up. — Week Days.

	Central Station,	mrn	mrn	mrn	mrn	mrn	mrn	aft	mrn	aft	aft	aft	aft		aft	aft	aft
Miles from Manchester (Cen.)	680 LIVERPOOL ....dep.	....	5 10	6 15	....	7 45	....	....	10 5	1030	1255			1 30	Saturdays only.	2 35	2 35
	680 SOUTHPORT (Lord St.) ,,	....	....	....	....	....	....	8 50	9 0		1040			1225		1 25	1 25
	680 WARRINGTON (Cen.). ,,	....	5 48	6 55	....	7 55	....	9 55	1055	1 20				1 55		3 0	3 0
761	BLACKPOOL { Central dep.	....	....	....	5550	....	8 25	....		1020						1245	1245
767	{ T. Road ,,	....	....	....	6 28	....	7 1 5	8 30		1043						1 7	1 7
775	BLACKBURN ,,	....	....	....	7 20	....	7 43	9 38		1215			1255			1 50	1 50
564	BOLTON (Trinity St.) ,,	....	....	....	8 0	....	7 52	9 58		1247			1 40			3 25	3 25
	MANCHESTER (Vic.) § ,,	....	....	....		....	8 40	1043		1 15							
8	Manchester (Cen.) ¶ ....dep.	....	6 32	7 50	....	8 30	8 55	1055	1120	1 50		1 53	2 45		Thursdays and Saturdays.	3 25
9	Cheadle Heath........... ,,	....	6 55	8 4	....	8s18	8 57	1110	1 44			2 20				
14	Stockport .... ,,	....	6 59	....	....	8 35	9 21	1011	1142	1 1						3 29
17¾	Marple .... ,,	....	7 14	....	....	8 47	9 33	11 9	1155	1 41		2 18				3 20
19¾	New Mills .... ,,	....	7 22	....	....	9 42	....		1 26			2 28				3 34
	Chinley ¶ .... ,,	....	7 33	8 32	....	9 19	9 51	1123	1182	1210	2 37	2 48			3 57
—	Mls Buxton......[Dale dep.	....	7 26	8 15	....	8 45	9 15	1110		1 35		1450	1450			
6¾	Peak Forest, for Peak ,,	....	....	....	....	....	9 32	1123	1135	1 48						
10¾	Chapel-en-le-Frith † ,,	....	7 43	8 33	....	9 3	9 41	1130	1142	1 55						
12½	Chinley .... arr.	....	7 46	8 36	....	9 9	9 46	1133	1146	1 58		2 32	2 32			
—	Chinley.............dep.	....	7 55	8 40	....	9 12	10 2	1140		1212	2 26	2 30	2 49	2 51		4 14
25¾	Edale .... ,,	7 35	8 8	8 53	....	....	10 15	....		1225		2 45	2 53	6		
30¾	Hope †† .... ,,	7 43	8 16	9 1	....	a	10 23	....		1233		2 53	1 3	14		4 43
32	Bamford .... ,,	7 47	8 20	9 5	....	....	10 27	....		1237		2 57	3	18		4 47
33¾	Hathersage .... ,,	7 52	8 25	9 10	....	....	10 32	....		1242		3 2	3 10	3 23		4 52
35¾	Grindleford .... ,,	7 56	8 29	9 14	....	....	10 36	....		1246		3 6	3 14	3 27		4 56
40¾	Dore and Totley 548 .. arr.	8 3	8 37	....	9 45	....	10 44	1211		1254		3 14		3 35	3 46		5 4
48¾	548 CHESTERFIELD .....arr.	8 52	9m40	10s27	....	1027	11 17	1256		1 33	3c43	3 43		4 13	4 12	5c24c	5244
72¾	548 DERBY .... ,,	8 57	10s23	11s22	....	....	12 20	....		2 22		4 43		5 7		6c10	6245
113¾	549 BIRMINGHAM (NewSt) ,,	1016	11m48	1 k7	....	....	1 35	....		3 20		5 35		6 45		7c20	8252
77	549 NOTTINGHAM ...... ,,	1625	10s33	12s18	....	....	1 15	....		2c58		5s30		6 10			7 2
94	549 LEICESTER (Lon. Rd.) ,,	....	1015	....	....	....	12s22	....		3 55		6 20		6c20			7053
193½	549 LONDON (St. Pan.) .. ,,	....	12 c5	....	....	....	2c10	....		5c2s		8 15		8c15			10 0
—	Dore and Totley ....dep.	8 4	8 38	....	9 46	....	10 45	1212		1255		3 15		3 36	3 47		5 5
41½	Beauchief and Abbey Dale.. ,,	8 8	....	....	....	....	....	....		1259		3 18					5 8
42½	Mill Houses and Ecclesall .. ,,	8 11	....	....	....	....	....	....		1 2		3 21					5 11
43½	Heeley .... ,,	8 14	8 44	9 28	....	....	10 52	....		1 6		3 25		3 42	3 54	d	d	5 14
45	Sheffield ** 539, 608 .. arr.	8 18	8 48	9 32	....	9 55	10 55	1221		1 9		3 29		3 47	3 58	4 35	4 45	5 18
50½	Rotherham (Masboro') ,,	8 32	9 20	....	....	....	....	1250		1s56		3 33		4 4				
51	,, (Westgate) ,,	....	....	10 16	....	1016	11 21	....		....				4 28		5 8	5	5 46
114½	793 HULL (Cannon St.) .. arr.	....	11 40	....	....	....	....	4 10				6 10		6 10				
115	726 HULL (Paragon)...... ,,	1056	....	11 27	....	....	2 4	....		4 11		6 53		6 55	6 55		6 55	6 55
9¼	539 YORK .... ,,	9 30	10 42	....	....	....	12 33	2 27		3 A0		5 38		5 38	5 38	7 0	7	7 27
172	684 NEWCASTLE (Central) ,,	11 7	1054	....	....	....	2 45	5 3		5 25		7 55		7 55	7 55			

Up. — Week Days—Continued. / Sundays.

Central Station,	aft	aft		aft	aft	aft	aft	aft	aft		aft		aft	mrn	non	mrn	aft	aft	aft	aft
680 LIVERPOOL ....dep.	3 30	3 30		4 0	....	4 30	5 30	6 30	7 30		8 35		8 30	....	....	1115	....	6 10		
680 SOUTHPORT (L. St.). ,,	1 25	2 50		....	....	....	4 5	....	5 25		7 15		7 15	....	....	....	....	....		
680 WARRINGTON (Cen.) ,,	3 0	3 55		4 27	....	4 55	5 55	6 55	7 55		9 5		8 55	....	....	1118	....	6 37		
761 BLACKPOOL { Cen...dep.	1H58	1H58		....	....	....	....	....	....		....		....	....	....	8 5	....	1 15		
{ T. Road ,,	1 37	1 37		3 45	2 25	....	4 20	....	....		....		....	....	....	7 30	....	1 37		
767 BLACKBURN ...... ,,	2 44	2 44		....	....	....	4 10	....	5 20		....		....	....	....	11 0	....	2 3		
775 BOLTON (Trin. St.).. ,,	3 25	3 25		3 54	3 54	....	4 40	....	....		....		....	....	....	1131	....	3 45		
564 MANCHESTER (V.) §.. ,,	4 24	2		4 40	4 40	....	5 38	....	4 17		....		....	....	....	12 5	....	4 15		
Manchester (Cen.) ¶ ..dep.	4 20	4 50		....	5 30	....	....	6 35	7 20	8 25		9 0		9 30	8 15	12 0	....	6 55	
Cheadle Heath .... ,,	....	5 4		....	5 20	....	....	6 48	....	8 42		9 30		....	8 42	12 4	....	7 13	
Stockport........... ,,	3 29	....		5 5	5 3	....	....	....	7 43	8s25		....		8 42	12 4	....	7 13	
Marple .... ,,	4 29	4 39		5 15	5 15	....	6 12	....	7 55	8s36		....		8 56	1231	....	7 13	
New Mills .... ,,	4 38	4 38		5 47	5 31	5 59	6 26	....	7p10	8s45		....		9 5	1240	....	7 13	
Chinley ¶ .... arr.	4 53	5 26		5 31	5 59	6 26	....	7 14	9 9	4		9 53		10 3	9 17	1238	1249	7 37	
Buxton ....[Dale dep.	4 d5	4 52		5d12		5d12	5s35	6 45	7 30	....		9 d8		9 d8	8d25	....	....	7d10	
Peak Forest, for Peak ,,	....	5 5		....		....	6 10	6 58	7 43	....		....		9 2	....	....	....		
Chapel-en-le-Frith †.. ,,	4 45	5 12		5 43		5 43	6 18	....	7 50	....		9 41		9 10	....	....	....	6 55	
Chinley .... arr.	4 45	5 15		5 50		5 50	6 31	....	7 53	....		9 44		9 13	....	....	....	6 58	
Chinley.............dep.	4 59	5 29		5 50	6 4	6 31	....	7 16	9 13	9 6		9 56		10 6	9 21	1 0	....	7 50	8 5
Edale .... ,,	....	5 42		....	6 17	....	....	....	8 26	9 20		....		9 34	....	....	1 18	3 8	8 18
Hope †† .... ,,	....	5 50		....	6 25	....	....	....	8 34	9 28		....		9 42	1 18	1 35	5	8 11	8 26
Bamford .... ,,	....	5 54		....	6 29	....	....	....	8 38	9 32		....		9 46	....	1 39	5	4 8 15	8 30
Hathersage .... ,,	....	5 59		....	6 34	....	....	....	8 43	9 37		....		9 51	....	1 44	5	9 8 20	8 35
Grindleford .... ,,	....	6 3		....	6 38	....	....	....	8 47	9 41		....		9 55	....	1 48	5	1 5 8 24	8 39
Dore and Totley 548.. arr.	5 30	6 11		....	6 46	....	....	....	8 55	9 49		1027		1037	10 3	....	1 56	5 21	8 32	8 47
548 CHESTERFIELD ..... ,,	6 0	7 c1		....	7 24	....	....	8s38	5 42	1025		1130		1130	1115	c	....	2 26	18 29	
548 DERBY .... ,,	....	....		....	8 25	....	....	h1025	1225	....		....		1145	c	....	6 57	2218	
549 BIRMINGHAM (N.St.) ,,	....	....		....	9 42	....	....	....	....	....		....		1248	c	....	8 32	8 322	
549 NOTTINGHAM ...... ,,	....	8c20		....	8c45	....	....	1115	1158	....		....		1235	c	....	7 27	27 40	
549 LEICESTER (L. Rd.) .. ,,	....	8c30		....	9c23	....	....	1157	1 42			1 42		1c57	....	....	7 38	8 531	
549 LONDON (St. Pan.).. ,,	....	....		....	1025c	....	....	....	4 20			4 20		4c30	....	....	9 50	1010	
Dore and Totley .....dep.	5 31	6 12		....	6 47	....	....	8 56	9 50			1028		1037	10 4	....	1 57	5 22	8 33	8 48
Beauchief and Abbey Dale. ,,	....	....		....	....	....	....	8 59	....			....		10 8	....	....	2 15	26 8	
Mill Houses and Ecclesall. ,,	....	....		....	....	....	....	9 2	....			....		1011	....	....	2 45	29 8	
Heeley .... ,,	5 39	6 18		6 25	6 55	7 10	....	7 51	9 6	9 56		1035		1045	1014	1 38	2 7	32 8	
Sheffield ** 539, 608 arr.	5 43	6 22		6 30	7 0	7 15	....	7 55	9 10	10 0		1040		1050	1018	1 42	2 12	37 8	
Rotherham (Masboro') ,,	6 3	7 10		7 10	7 26	....	....	8 37	9239	....		....		....	1 18	....	2 46	22 9	
,, (Westgte) ,,	....	....		....	7 48	....	....	....	1019			11 4		1133	....	2 8	....	....	
793 HULL (Cannon St.).. arr.	9 18	....		9 18	1020	1020	....	1020	....	6 30		6 30		6 30	....	....	6 14	....	
726 HULL (Paragon)..... ,,	10 9	....		....	1136	1136	....	1136	....	4 42		4 42		4 42	....	....	9 13	4 42	4 42
539 YORK .... ,,	7 45	....		7 45	10 5	10 5	....	10 51	36 3	31		3 31		3 31	....	....	5 22	3 31	3 31
684 NEWCASTLE (Central) ,,	1016	....		....	1232	1232	....	1232	1428	5 58		5 58		5 58	....	....	5 5	5 58	5 58

a Sets down from Manchester and the Cheshire Lines.
A Arrives at 2 36 aft. on Mondays, Fridays, and Saturdays.
b Stops on Wednesdays.
b Except Mondays.
B Arrives at 2 13 aft. on Saturdays.
c Via Sheffield.
d Stops to set down from beyond Chinley.
d Via Miller's Dale.
e Except Saturdays.
g Arrives at 5 8 aft. on Wednesdays.
h Arrives at 10 37 aft. on Saturdays.

H Leaves at 1 15 aft. until 9th instant.
i Arrives at 2 53 mrn. on Sundays.
k Via Heeley.
l Mondays only.
n Via Sheffield ; arrives Chesterfield at 9 32, Derby 10 3, and Birmingham 11 17 mrn. on Mondays.
N Leaves at 2 43 aft. on and after the 23rd instant.
o Via Leeds.
p Leaves at 7 43 aft. on Saturdays.
q Arrives Chesterfield at 5 24, Derby at 6 10, Birmingham at 7 20, and Leicester at 7 40 aft. on Thursdays.

r Leaves at 8 12 mrn. on Mondays.
s Saturdays only.
t Arrives at 10 1 aft. on Thursdays and Saturdays.
v Arrives at 9 55 aft. on Saturdays.
x Leaves at 9 15 mrn. on Saturdays.

† Over 1 mile to L & N. W. Station.
§ Via Marple.
** ½ mile to Victoria Station, G.C.
†† Station for Castleton (2 miles) and Bradwell (2 miles).

July 1910

MANCHESTER, CHINLEY, HATHERSAGE, and SHEFFIELD

Miles		Week Days																				Sundays						
		a.m	a.m		a.m	a.m		a.m		p.m	p.m S (Commences 26th June)	p.m	p.m S (Runs 19th June to 28th August inclusive)	p.m S	p.m E		p.m		p.m	p.m		a.m	a.m		p.m	p.m	p.m	p.m
	Manchester (Cen.) .. dep	..	6 5	..	..	9 0	..	11 35	..	1 50	B	3 55	D	4 34	5 22	..	5 50	..	7 35	9 35	..	9 0	10 8	..	2 0	..	6 40	[illegible] 5
	Stockport (T.D.) .... "	..	6 34	..	..	8 58	..	11 20	..	1 33	..	4 23	..	4 51	5F36	..	..	—	7T49	9 55	..	8 55	10 35	..	1 50	..	7 8	8 24
19¾	Chinley .... "	7 12	7 41	..	..	9 50	..	12 30	..	2 35	2†50	5 6	5†32	5 40	6 5	..	6 31	..	8 22	1040	..	9 55	11 12	..	2 48	..	8 8	9 8
25¼	Edale	7 26	7 56	..	..	10 4	..	12 44	..	2 49	..	5 19	..	5 54	6 19	..	6 45	..	8 35	1054	..	1011	11 27	..	3 3	..	8 24	9 23
30¼	Hope A	7 34	8 4	..	9 0	1012	..	12 52	..	2 57	..	5 27	..	6 2	6 27	..	6 53	..	8 43	11 2	..	1020	11 35	..	3 11	6 50	8 32	9 31
32	Bamford	7 38	8 8	..	9 5	1016	..	12 56	..	3 1	..	5 33	..	6 6	6 31	..	6 57	..	8 47	11 6	..	1024	11 39	..	3 16	6 54	8 36	9 35
33¾	Hathersage	7 42	8 13	..	9 10	1020	..	1 0	..	3 5	..	5 37	..	6 10	6 35	..	7 1	..	8 51	1110	..	1030	11 44	..	3 20	7 0	8 41	9 41
35¾	Grindleford	7 47	8 18	..	9 15	1025	..	1 5	..	3 10	..	5 42	..	6 15	6 40	..	7 6	..	8 56	1115	..	1036	11 49	..	3 25	7 6	8 46	9 47
40¾	Dore and Totley	7 56	8 27	..	9 24	1034	..	1 14	..	3 19	3†33	5 51	6†10	6 24	6 49	..	7 15	..	9 5	1124	..	1045	11 58	..	3 35	7 15	8 55	9 57
48¾	247 Chesterfield ...... arr	8 32	8 49	..	..	1255	..	2U31	..	4 34	4 34	6 26	..	7 30	7 30	..	..	..	9 39	..	..	..	..	..	4 34	..	..	1034
69¾	234 Mansfield 239 .... "	..	..	..	..	..	..	6EC28	..	..	..	..	..	..	..	..	..	..	..	..	..	..	..	..	..	..	..	..
41½	Beauchief	..	..	..	..	1037	..	1 17	..	3 22	..	5 54	..	6 27	..	..	7 18	..	9 8	..	..	..	..	..	..	..	..	..
42½	Millhouses & Ecclesall ..	..	..	..	9 28	1040	..	1 20	..	3 25	..	5 57	..	6 30	..	..	7 21	..	9 11	..	..	1049	..	..	..	7 18	8 59	10 1
43½	Heeley	8 3	8 33	..	9 32	1044	..	1 24	..	3 29	..	6 1	..	6 34	6 55	..	7 25	..	9 15	1130	..	1053	..	..	3 41	7 23	9 3	10 5
45	Sheffield .... arr	8 7	8 37	..	9 36	1051	..	1 31	..	3 33	3 45	6 5	6 20	6 38	7 0	..	7 29	..	9 20	1136	..	1057	12 6	..	3 45	7 28	9 7	1010

Miles		Week Days																				Sundays							
		a.m	a.m	a.m	a.m	a.m S (Runs 19th June to 28th August inclusive)	a.m S (Runs 19th June to 18th September inclusive)	a.m		p.m		p.m S		p.m S	p.m	p.m	p.m E		p.m	p.m		a.m	a.m	a.m		p.m		p.m	p.m
	Sheffield .... dep	6 0	7 2	7 45	8 8	8 40	1010	1050	..	1240	..	1 11	..	2 22	4 30	5 30	6 25	..	7 0	9 25	..	8 30	9 0	10 0	..	2 0	..	6 10	7 5
1½	Heeley	6 5	7 8	7 50	..	H	K	1055	..	1245	..	1 16	..	2 28	4 35	5 36	6 30	..	7 6	9 30	..	8 36	9 6	10 6	..	2 7	..	6 16	..
2¼	Millhouses & Ecclesall ..	..	7 14	7 55	..	..	..	11 0	..	1250	..	..	..	2 34	4 40	5 42	..	..	7 12	..	..	8 42	9 12	1012	..	2 13	..	6 22	..
3½	Beauchief	..	..	7 58	..	..	..	11 3	..	..	..	..	..	2 38	4 43	..	..	..	..	..	..	..	..	..	..	..	..	..	..
—	239 Mansfield 234 .... dep	..	..	..	..	..	5C56	5C56	..	..	..	..	..	..	..	..	..	..	..	..	..	..	..	..	..	..	..	..	..
—	247 Chesterfield ...... "	..	6 53	7 29	..	..	9 45	8N2	..	..	..	..	..	1 42	3‡38	5 13	5 45	..	..	8 33	..	8 3	..	..	..	..	..	5 50	..
4¼	Dore and Totley	6 13	7 20	8 2	..	..	1020	11 6	..	1256	..	1 24	..	2 42	4 46	5 48	6 38	..	7 18	9 38	..	8 53	9 19	1018	..	2 20	..	6 28	..
9¼	Grindleford	6 25	7 33	8 13	..	..	..	1117	..	1 8	..	1 35	..	2 54	4 57	6 0	6 49	..	7 30	9 49	..	9 5	9 31	1030	..	2 32	..	6 40	7 24
11¼	Hathersage	6 32	7 38	8 18	..	..	..	1122	..	1 14	..	1 40	..	2 59	5 2	6 5	6 54	..	7 35	9 54	..	9 11	9 37	1035	..	2 37	..	6 45	7 29
13	Bamford	6 37	7 43	8 22	..	..	..	1126	..	1 18	..	1 44	..	3 4	5 6	6 10	6 58	..	7 40	9 58	..	9 16	9 43	1040	..	2 42	..	6 50	..
14¾	Hope A	6 44	7 49	8 27	8 35	..	..	1132	..	1 24	..	1 50	..	3 10	5 12	6 16	7 4	..	7 46	10 4	..	9 23	9 48	1046	..	2 48	..	6 57	7 37
19½	Edale	6 57	8 2	..	8 48	..	..	1144	..	1 36	..	2 2	..	3 23	5 24	6 29	7 16	..	7 59	10 16	..	9 36	..	1059	..	3 1	..	7 10	7 50
25¼	Chinley .... arr	7 8	8 13	..	8 59	9 33	11 0	1155	..	1 47	..	2 13	..	3 34	5 35	6 40	7 27	..	8 10	10 27	..	9 47	..	1110	..	3 12	..	7 21	8 1
37¼	Stockport (T.D.) .... "	7H54	8L45	..	9Z38	..	..	1 20	..	3 35	..	3 35	..	..	6 18	7 13	..	..	8J33	10K48	..	1026	..	1156	..	3 57	..	7 54	8 45
45	Manchester (Cen.) .. "	8 8	8 59	..	9 24	..	.	1 15	..	2 50	..	2 50	..	..	6 44	7 39	..	..	8 55	11 10	..	1057	..	1225	..	4 25	..	8 23	9 8

A For Castleton (2 miles) and Bradwell
B Through Carriages from Llandudno dep. 11 35 a.m. (Tables 99 and 211)
C Via Chesterfield and Pye Bridge
D Through Carriages from Blackpool (North) dep. 2 45 p.m. (Tables 160 and 211)
E or E Except Saturdays
F Cheadle Heath (Stockport) Passengers can dep. Tiviot Dale 4 51 p.m

H Through Carriages to Blackpool (North) arr. 11 58 a.m. (Tables 211 and 160)
H Cheadle Heath (Stockport)
J Cheadle Heath (Stockport). Passengers can arrive Tiviot Dale 8 52 p.m.
K Through Carriages to Llandudno arr. 1 57 p.m. (Tables 211 and 99)
K Cheadle Heath (Stockport). Passengers can arrive Tiviot Dale 11 5 p.m.

L Cheadle Heath (Stockport). Passengers can arrive Tiviot Dale 8 48 a.m.
N Dep. 9 45 a.m. on Saturdays
S or S Saturdays only
T Cheadle Heath (Stockport). Passengers can depart Tiviot Dale 7 11 p.m.
U Arr. 1 44 p.m on Saturdays
Z Passengers can arr. Cheadle Heath (Stockport) at 9 55 a.m

† Stops to set down only
‡ 5 mins. later on Saturdays

July 1948

June 1964

SHEFFIELD AND CHINLEY

Miles		WEEKDAYS												
		a.m.	a.m.	SX p.m. (T.C. from Manchester Central dep 8.45 a.m.)	SO a.m. (T.C. from Manchester Central dep. 8.45 a.m.)	p.m. (T.C. from Manchester Central dep. 11.45 a.m.)	SO p.m. (Commences 27th June; T.C. from Llandudno dep. 11.30 a.m.)	p.m. (T.C. from Manchester Central dep. 1.45 p.m.)	SX p.m. (T.C. from Manchester Central dep. 3.30 p.m.)	SX p.m. (T.C. from Manchester Central dep. 4.10 p.m.)	SO p.m. (T.C. from Manchester Central dep. 4.10 p.m.)	SO p.m.	p.m.	p.m. (T.C. from Manchester Central dep. 7.22 p.m.)
0	**CHINLEY** ... ... dep.	7 0	7 40	9 42	9 58	12 55	...	2 55	4 24	5 8	5 12	5 40	6 32	8 40
5¾	Edale	7 13	7 53	9 55	10 11	1 6	.	3 8	4 35	5 21	5 25	5 53	6 45	8 53
10¾	Hope (for Castleton & Bradwell) ...	7 21	8 2	10 3	10 19	1 13	3b 2	3 16	4 42	5 29	5 33	6 1	6 53	9 1
12¼	Bamford	7 25	8 6	10 7	10 23	1 17	.	3 20	4 46	5 33	5 37	6 5	6 57	9 5
14½	Hathersage	7 29	8 10	10 11	10 27	1 22	...	3 24	4 51	5 37	5 41	6 9	7 1	9 9
16½	Grindleford	7 34	8 15	10 16	10 32	1 26	.	3 29	4 55	5 42	5 46	6 14	7 6	9 14
21½	Dore and Totley	7 43	8 24	10 25	10 41	1 34	3b24	3 38	5 3	5 51	5 55	6 23	7 16	9 23
	CHESTERFIELD Midland arr.	8A 8	8SX45	.	.	.	4 39	4 39	5 57	6 19	6 19	.	8 10	9B50
22¾	Millhouses and Ecclesall	7 48	...	10 30	10 46	1 39	...	3 43	5 8	5 56	6 0	6 27	7 21	9 28
24	Heeley	7 52	8 31	10 34	10 50	1 43	3b32	3 47	5 12	6 0	6 4	6 31	7 25	9 32
25½	**SHEFFIELD** Midland ... arr.	7 58	8 37	10 40	10 56	1 51	3 38	3 53	5 19	6 6	6 10	6 38	7 31	9 38

	W'DAYS. — contd.		SUNDAYS									
	SX p.m. (T.C. from Manchester Central dep. 9.30 p.m.)	SO p.m. (T.C. from Manchester Central dep. 9.30 p.m.)	a.m. (T.C. from Manchester Central dep. 8.40 a.m.)	a.m. (T.C. from Liverpool Lime Street dep. 9.30 a.m.)	p.m.	p.m. (T.C. from Liverpool Lime Street dep. 4.30 p.m.)	p.m.		p.m.		p.m.	
CHINLEY ... ... dep.	10 42	10 42	9 50	11 23	3 15	6 14	6 25	...	7 5	...	8 25	...
Edale	.	10 56	10 1	11 35	3 28		6 38	.	7 18	.	8 38	.
Hope (for Castleton & Bradwell) ...	...	11 4	10 7	11 42	3 36		6 46	...	7 26	...	8 46	...
Bamford	.	11 8	10 11	11 45	3 40		6 50	.	7 30	.	8 50	.
Hathersage	...	11 13	10 15	11 51	3 44		6 54	...	7 34	...	8 54	...
Grindleford	.	11 18	10 19	11 55	3 49		6 59	.	7 39	.	8 59	.
Dore and Totley	...	...	...	...	...		...	...	...	...	...	...
CHESTERFIELD Midland arr.	.	.	.	.	.		.	.	.	.	.	.
Millhouses and Ecclesall	...	...	...	...	...		...	...	...	...	...	...
Heeley	.	.	10 34	.	4 4		7 14	.	7 54	.	9 14	.
SHEFFIELD Midland ... arr.	11 27	11 38	10 40	12 10	4 10	6 51	7 20	...	8 1	...	9 20	...

‡—Stops to pick up passengers only
b—Stops only to set down passengers
A—On Saturdays arrives 8.7 a.m.
B—On Saturdays arrives 9.58 p.m.
SO—Saturdays only
SX—Saturdays excepted
TC—Through Carriages

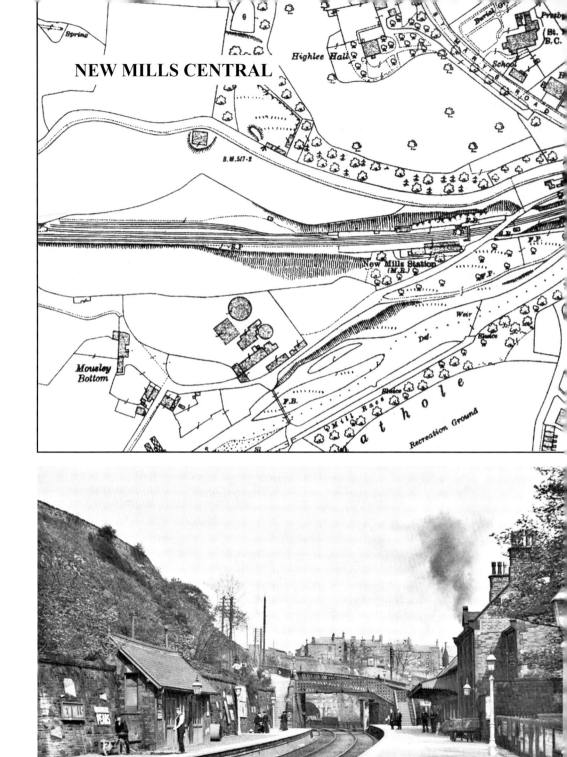

NEW MILLS CENTRAL

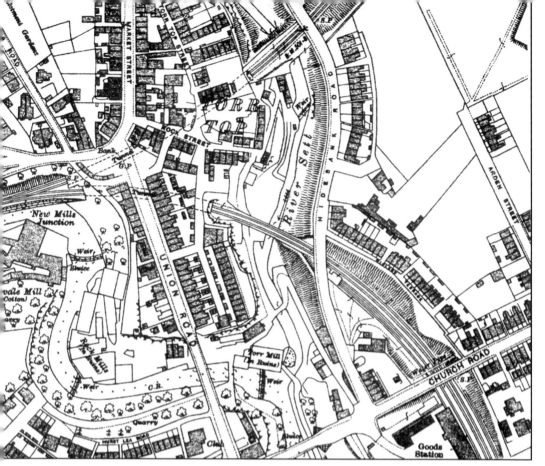

II. The 1919 edition has the station on the left page together with three sidings and the gas works. The latter received its coal from barges on the nearby River Goyt. One of the sidings remained for reversal purposes in 2020. On the right page is the junction plus two tunnels and part of the goods yard, which closed on 9th September 1968. It is lower right. To the left of it is Torr Mill, which was destroyed by fire in 1912. Near it now stands a 12 tonne Archimedes screw capable of producing 63kW of electricity.

→ III. The 1913 RCH diagram reveals the five route destinations. We will run on the joint line to Derby, as far as Chinley Junction.

← 1. We are near the centre of the left page of the map, looking east. Beyond the footbridge is the signal box and the southern tunnel portal. The high ground is known as The Torrs. The first box was in use from 1877 until 1st November 1924. The map contains TORR TOP, near the River Sett. (J.Alsop coll.)

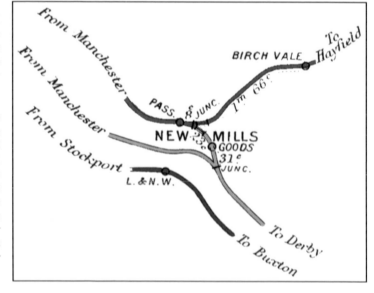

2.   A fine postcard record includes three of the six chimneys deemed necessary for the 1864 house for the station master, which is on the right. The waiting room on the left appears to have two, plus a gas lamp. The short train is probably bound for Hayfield. (R.Humm coll.)

3.   A vista from the platform end includes both tunnel mouths and signals for both routes. The box had 30 levers and was still in use in 2020. The train departing on 27th June 1948 is bound for Hayfield. The population of New Mills was 6253 in 1901 and 8710 in 1961. (SLS coll.)

4.   Approaching Hayfield Tunnel on 21st April 1951 is 4-4-2T no. 67412. This class C13 was introduced in 1903 and a few were fitted for push-pull working. On the right is New Mills Tunnel, which was 123yds in length. There was a 10-lever signal box at its far end from 16th December 1924 until 5th January 1970. (J.Suter coll.)

5.   Here, we have a westward panorama from 2nd June 1955. The term 'Central' was added on 25th August 1952 to the station and in 1977 to the signal box. The two sidings for exchange traffic are in the distance, together with a crossover for use by terminating trains. The semaphore signals lasted until 2007, when colour lights appeared. There was a crash here in 1867 involving 27 loaded cattle wagons, plus three carriages. The fatalities were mainly sheep, but included four drovers. (R.Humm coll.)

6. A four-car Trans-Pennine unit, with vehicle E51953 leading, heads east from New Mills Central on 26th March 1981. The track diverging in the foreground is the former Hayfield branch. This was still used as a reversing siding for local trains from Manchester in the 1980s. Included is Torvale Cotton Mill and the River Sett, which flows westwards across map II. In 2020, the booking office on platform 1 was staffed six days per week, from early morning until early afternoon. (P.D.Shannon)

← 7. Arriving in August 1982 with a Skegness to Manchester service is no. 40061, an English Electric 1Co-Co1. On the left, a DMU waits on the short siding to reverse to Manchester. This crossover was later removed, leaving the one west of the platforms in use in 2020. (J.Whitehouse)

New Mills Newtown station is in the *Buxton to Stockport* album of our Northern Line series; pictures 80 to 85. It was still in use in 2020.

Hayfield Branch
BIRCH VALE

IV. The River Sett runs westwards, close to the single line branch, shown at 2ins to 1 mile on this 1947 map. After closure, the route became the Sett Valley Trail. The Pennine Bridleway also passes through Birch Vale. The district is known as the Dark Peak.

↓ 8. The curved row of cottages was built in the 1830s for workers at the print works nearby. On the right is the station, which was open for passengers until 5th January 1970 and goods until 2nd November 1964. (J.Alsop coll.)

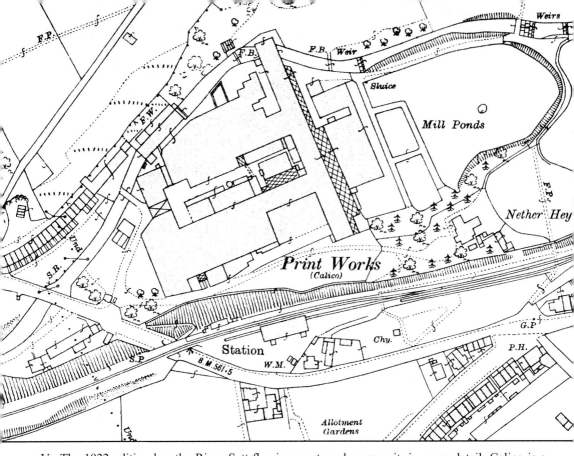

V. The 1922 edition has the River Sett flowing westwards across it, in more detail. Calico is a cotton cloth good at accepting coloured patterns on it.

9. Class C14 4-4-2T no. 67448 waits with a train from Hayfield on 21st April 1955. There was a 30cwt crane listed here in 1938 and a signal box from 19th February 1889 until 4th December 1910. (J.Suter coll.)

HAYFIELD

10.   We are looking towards the end of the line in this early postcard and have the well-ventilated facilities for gentlemen on the left. The train will have just run over Slacks Crossing, which had a signal box until 13th November 1927. (P.Laming coll.)

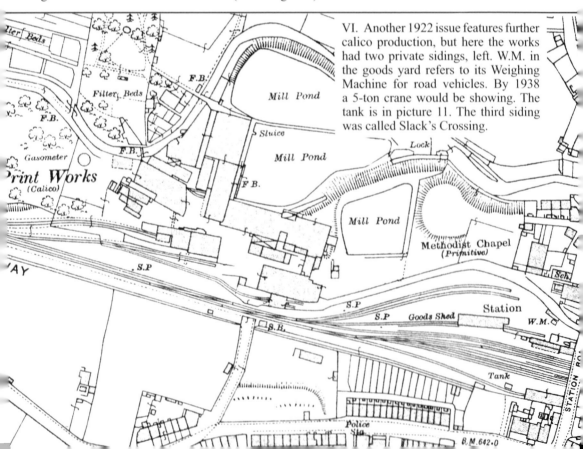

VI. Another 1922 issue features further calico production, but here the works had two private sidings, left. W.M. in the goods yard refers to its Weighing Machine for road vehicles. By 1938 a 5-ton crane would be showing. The tank is in picture 11. The third siding was called Slack's Crossing.

11. The engine shed is seen on 9th March 1952 and present is no. 67401, a class C13 4-4-2T, a type used widely in this area since their introduction in 1903. The hut has a chimney for a stove for the benefit of the staff. The population in 1901 was 2614 and 2518 in 1961; mechanisation was reducing the need for labour. (J.Suter coll.)

12. On the left is the goods yard, which closed on 15th April 1963. Beyond it is the signal box. This had 20 levers and was worked from 20th January 1925 up to 5th January 1970, when the branch closed. Seen on 12th May 1956 running round its train is no. 67443, a class C14 4-4-2T. (J.Suter coll.)

13. The early DMUs were adorned with 'Cats' Whiskers' and provided with observation car visibility. On the left is the goods shed and the loading gauge. Gas lighting is in use, the works being just a little south of the station. After closure, the route became part of the Sett Valley Trail. (R.Humm coll.)

14. The prospective passenger's perspective is seen in 1965, with two DMUs present. In addition to calico, local industries included spinning, weaving, paper production, stone quarrying and millstone manufacture. Visitors to the Kinder Scout area at weekends were numerous. (Colour-Rail.com)

SOUTH OF NEW MILLS

15. Class 5 4-6-0 no. 44776 is running south on 8th July 1950, having bypassed New Mills, by running on the 1901 straight route from Hazel Grove. The lines to the former are to the right of the coaches. The route from the latter passes through Disley Tunnel, which has the great length of 2 miles 346yds. (Bentley coll.)

↓ 16. The 13.45 Manchester to Hull is passing on 11th September 1982. The Hazel Grove line is branching left beyond the signal box. The other end of it can be found in picture 101 in *Buxton to Stockport* and the 1986 connection to this former LNWR route is also shown in it. New Mills South Junction box opened on 14th June 1903 and had a new 55-lever frame provided in 1962. It was still in use in 2020. (T.Heavyside)

West of New Mills

HAZEL GROVE (MIDLAND)

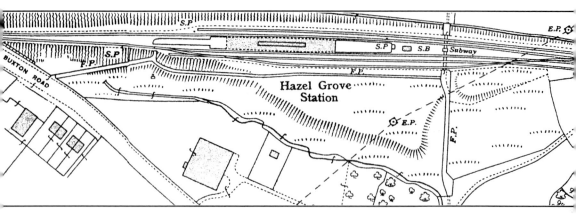

VIIa. This station was open from 1st July 1902 to 1st January 1917 and is shown on the 1936 edition. It had the suffix shown only in Bradshaw's index. Wartime economies brought many closures in 1917. To the west of its site is the present Hazel Grove station and the 1986 connection for trains on our route. This station was opened by the LNWR in 1857.

17. An island platform sufficed and the signal box is evident at the east end of it. The through lines were never closed; neither was the Low Level station. This can be found in pictures 98 to 100 of our *Buxton to Stockport* album; it includes the 1986 connection between the two Hazel Grove stations. (J.Alsop coll.)

Gowhole Sidings

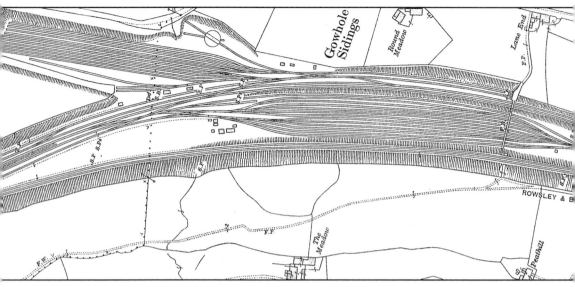

⬇ 18. Gowhole is about one mile south of New Mills on the opposite side of the river and canal from Furness Vale station, which was once LNWR property. The marshalling yard, or exchange sidings, were an MR creation by 1903. It is 21st April 1951 and no. 43612 is busy with four brake vans attached. It is a class 3F 0-6-0 of a type introduced by the MR in 1888. On the left is the signal box, which was in use from 19th December 1920 until 18th May 1969. The first box was named L&E Hall's Siding in about 1875. The name Gowhole Goods Junction was used at one period. This yard had been an extremely busy place. In the summer of 1953 for instance, more than 70 goods trains were scheduled to arrive and depart each day. Gowhole was in operation through the night. It finally closed in 1969 and was dismantled the following year. (J.Suter coll.)

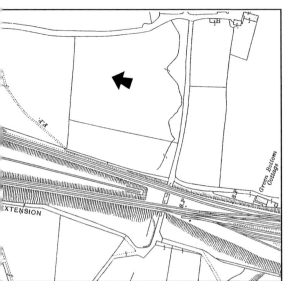

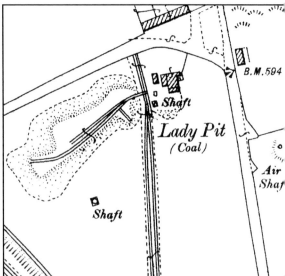

VIIb. The 1921 edition contains the northern part of the quadruple track finished in 1903. Top left are storage sidings, two of which had earlier served the closed coal mine called Lady Pit.

VIIc. The 1897 revision reveals that Lady Pit once had its own sidings. Its sinking started in 1816. It produced poor quality coal for limekilns and closed in 1903.

BUXWORTH

19. The station opened on 1st February 1867, shortly after the line. No public goods facilities were ever provided. This view east is from 1948. The distant signals on the left are for the lines that skirt the left of the platform, it being quadruple track here (Stations UK)

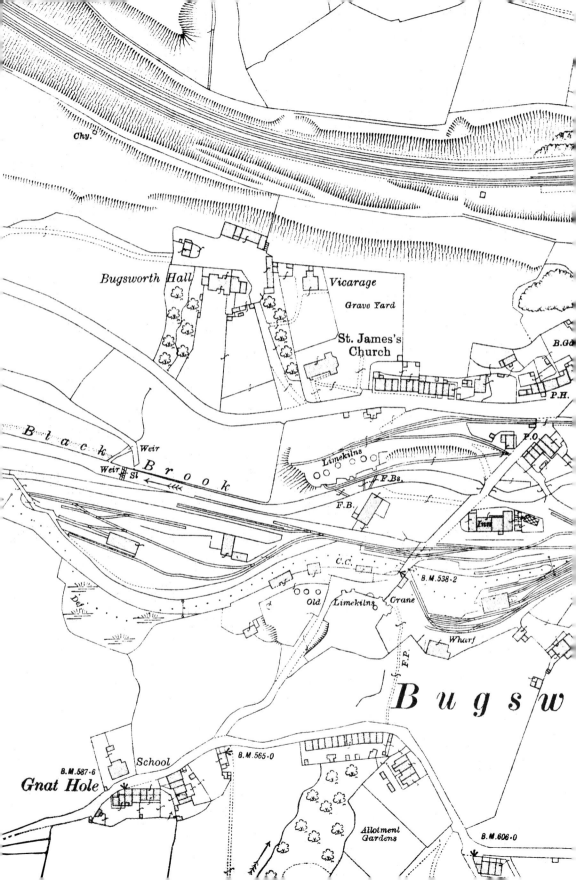

Chy.

Bugsworth Hall

Vicarage

Grave Yard

St. James's Church

B. Gd.

P. H.

Black

Brook

Weir

Weir St.

Limekilns

P.O.

F.Bs.

F.B.

Inn

C.C.

B.M.538·2

Def.

Old Limekilns

Crane

Wharf

F.P.

Bugsw

School

B.M.565·0

B.M.587·6

Gnat Hole

Allotment Gardens

B.M.606·0

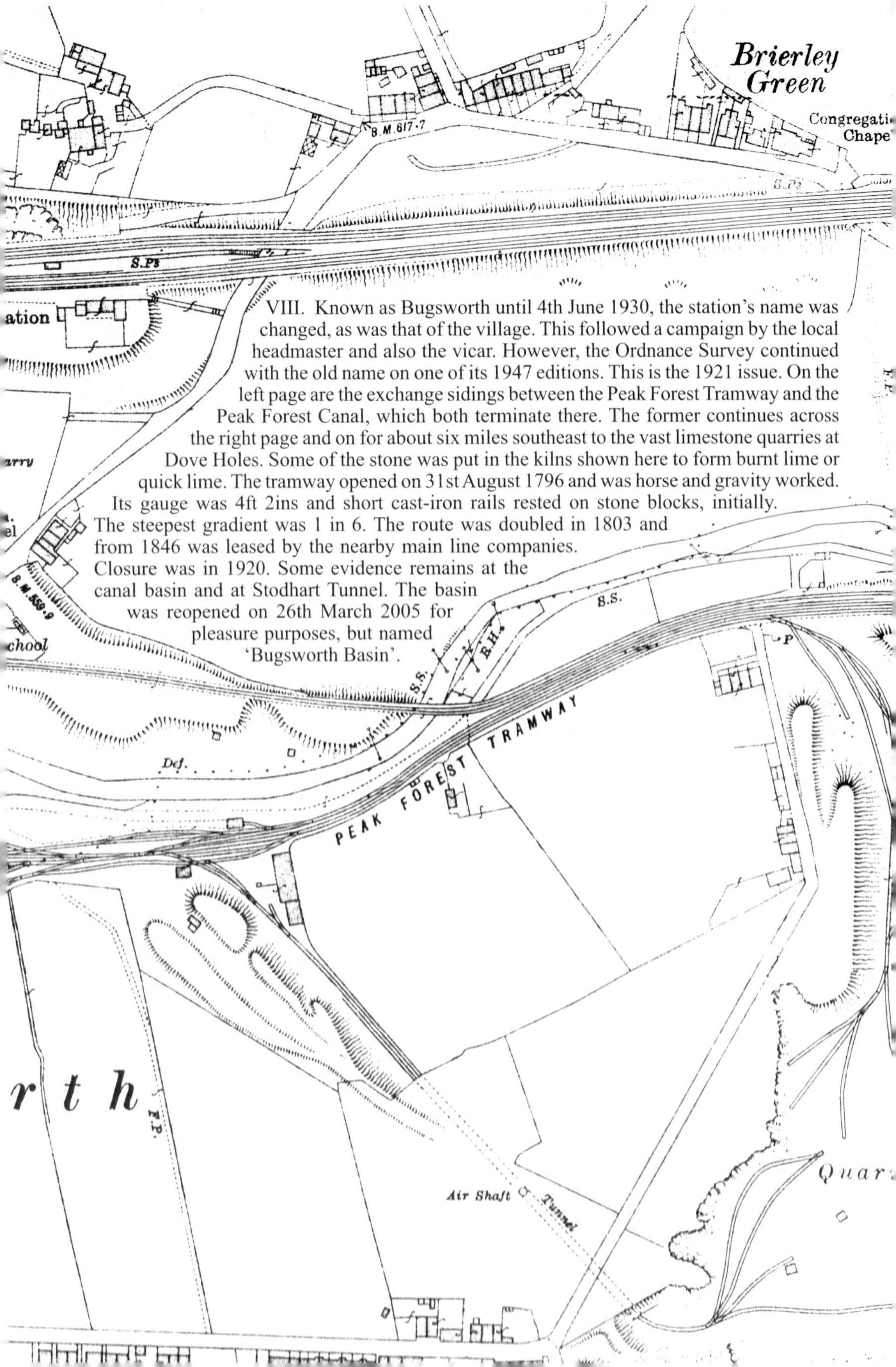

Congregati
Chape

B.M.617·7

S.Ps

S.Ps

ation

VIII. Known as Bugsworth until 4th June 1930, the station's name was
changed, as was that of the village. This followed a campaign by the local
headmaster and also the vicar. However, the Ordnance Survey continued
with the old name on one of its 1947 editions. This is the 1921 issue. On the
left page are the exchange sidings between the Peak Forest Tramway and the
Peak Forest Canal, which both terminate there. The former continues across
the right page and on for about six miles southeast to the vast limestone quarries at
Dove Holes. Some of the stone was put in the kilns shown here to form burnt lime or
quick lime. The tramway opened on 31st August 1796 and was horse and gravity worked.
Its gauge was 4ft 2ins and short cast-iron rails rested on stone blocks, initially.
The steepest gradient was 1 in 6. The route was doubled in 1803 and
from 1846 was leased by the nearby main line companies.
Closure was in 1920. Some evidence remains at the
canal basin and at Stodhart Tunnel. The basin
was reopened on 26th March 2005 for
pleasure purposes, but named
'Bugsworth Basin'.

arry

B.M.559·9

chool

S.S.

S.S.

B.H.

Def.

PEAK FOREST TRAMWAY

r t h

F.P.

Quar

Air Shaft   Tunnel

20.   Present on 29th July 1950 is 4-4-0 class 4P no. 41016, running towards Sheffield. The footpath on the right is shown on the map and to the north of it is a road going nowhere. It had been part of a plan to create another platform. (J.Suter coll.)

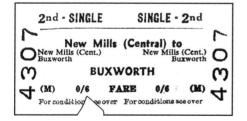

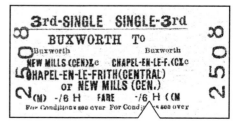

21. The cottages top left in this panorama from 2nd May 1953 are on Knowl Top. Running towards New Mills is class 4MT 2-6-4T no. 42306, a type introduced by the LMS in 1927. Evident is part of the quadruple track between New Mills and Chinley North Junction, completed in 1900 to 1903. A nearby tunnel was eliminated at that time. (J.Suter coll.)

22. It is 20th September 1958 and no. 44112 is passing a new colour light signal. The loco was a class 4F 0-6-0. New signal boxes arrived in 1876, 1884, 1893 and 1903; the last had 42 levers and closed on 29th September 1968. The station was closed on 15th September 1958 and was later used by the Burnage School for Boys, based in Manchester. (J.Suter coll.)

CHINLEY

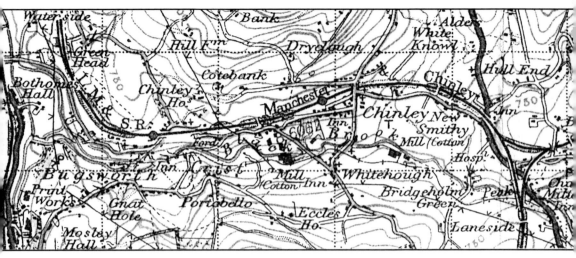

IX. The 1947 survey is shown at 2ins to 1 mile and has Chinley station below the 't' of Manchester. It retains part of the Peak Forest Tramway. The triangle on the right has Chinley North Junction top left, South Junction at the bottom and East Junction, plus our line to Edale, on the right.

Other views can be seen in *Buxton to Stockport* **(Northern Lines series) in pictures 40 to 43.**

23. The first station is seen in about 1900; it was just east of its successor, near the right of map X. The 1901 census recorded 1223 folk, but this included Bugsworth and Brownside. (P.Laming coll.)

24.   An early postcard includes a train at the bay platform, which was at the east end and was used by local trains. Refreshment rooms were included, as this became a busy junction station. By the early 1920s, the station was being served by 33 trains travelling in the Manchester direction and 35 heading south towards Derby and beyond, or east towards Sheffield. In 1922, 67,000 passengers bought tickets here.(P.Laming coll.)

X.   The 1919 issue is seen at 20ins to 1 mile and features the second station here, which opened on 1st June 1906.

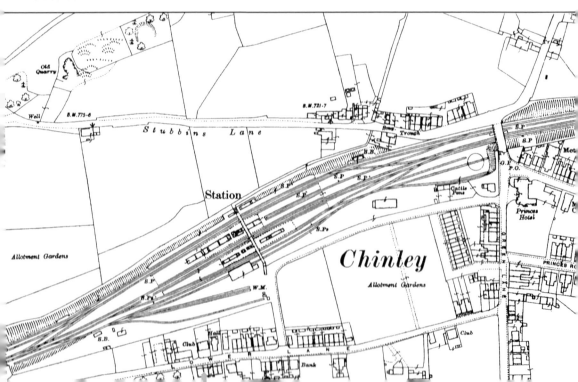

25.   Jubilee class 4-6-0 no. 45657 *Tyrwhitt* called at 9.40 on 10th July 1951, with the Manchester to St Pancras express. The coach near the turntable would be for engineering staff. The signal box is 'Chinley Station South Junction'. (J.Suter coll.)

26.   We move on to 17th May 1952 and witness class 4P 4-4-0 no. 40927 departing. The goods yard has a 5-ton crane near the shed; closure came on 7th October 1963. Upper quadrant signals have arrived. (J.Suter coll.)

27. An undated view westward includes the bay platform, new lights powered by electricity and second generation BR nameboards, often called 'Totems'. (M.J.Stretton coll.)

28. This is Chinley Station South Junction 1902 signal box. It had a new 48-lever frame in 1903 and was closed on 29th September 1968. It can also be seen in picture 25. (N.D.Mundy)

29.   The 14.15 Sheffield to Manchester departs on 20th July 1974. The running lines were reduced from four to two in the early 1980s. On the right is Chinley Station North Junction box. It had a 32-lever frame, which was in use from 22nd February 1902 until 6th December 1981. (T.Heavyside)

30.   It is 30th October 1992 and we see the two 6-car platforms. After the closure of the Matlock route, and the withdrawal of the Buxton branch passenger service, the station and trackwork were brutally rationalised. Here we see the remains from the station footbridge as Pacer unit no. 142061 departs with the 09.24 Sheffield-Manchester Piccadilly local service. A larger shelter was in place by 2017. (A.C.Hartless)

EAST OF CHINLEY

Chinley North Junction

➔ 31. The North Junction was recorded on 20th April 1965 as a class 8F 2-8-0 passes onto the Hope Valley line, with rusty coal wagons. The box opened on 26th October 1902 with a 44-lever frame. A new box with a panel came into use on 14th December 1980 and the name became simply 'Chinley'. (Colour-Rail.com)

⬇ 32. We see North Junction in the other direction in 1972, with a 10mph speed restriction to pass close to the box. Our Edale route is lower right and the Chapel-en-le-Frith lines are on the left. (R.Humm coll.)

➔ 33. The A624 was a convenient parking place on 14th July 1974 to stop close to North Junction. The train is carrying lime between Tunstead and Margam, but the southeast chord of the junction was out of use from 1964 to 1980. Thus the class 45 no. 45013 had to be uncoupled to allow it to run round its train. (T.Heavyside)

34. Running east on 12th May 1966 is no. 48327, an ex-LMS class 8F 2-8-0. Its short train appears to be for the benefit of engineers. The management have brought the joys of white ballast from local quarries. (Bentley coll.)

35. A 1963 photograph includes a third distant signal to tell express drivers the situation beyond the next home signal, in the Chinley area. The 16-lever framed box was in use from 29th October 1893 until 27th February 1966. (R.S.Carpenter coll.)

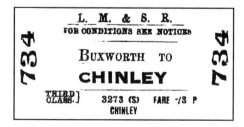

L. M. & S. R.
FOR CONDITIONS SEE NOTICES

734 BUXWORTH TO
CHINLEY 734

THIRD
CLASS.   3273 (S)   FARE -/3 P
CHINLEY

L. M. & S. R.
Issued subject to the conditions & regulations in the Cos Time Tables Books Bills & Notices and in the Railway Cos Book of regulations relating to traffic by Passenger train or other similar service

CHINLEY TO
BUXWORTH 6591

THIRD
CLASS   3270(S)   FARE -/2½
BUXWORTH

Cowburn Tunnel

36. Work began on the construction in October 1888 and the rails were laid by March 1893. This is the west portal soon after, when the tunnellers' temporary track and workshops were still in place over the tunnel. The breakthrough between the two ends took place on 18th July 1891. Cowburn West signal box was at the far end and it had 12 levers from 1893 to about 1966. (Bentley coll.)

37. This is the same location on 3rd May 1953 with class 4P 4-4-0 no. 41072 in action, 1¼ miles from Edale. The tunnel length is 2 miles 182yds. Its summit is about ½ mile from its eastern end. Only one vertical shaft was created. The signals were worked by Cowburn Tunnel East (also 12 levers) from 1894 to 3rd January 1957. (J.Suter coll.)

38. Cowburn Viaduct is over the River Noe and is seen on 20th May 1972, looking eastwards. There were two more overbridges to the hillside before reaching Edale. The peak is at Kinder Scout, 2088ft above sea level, two miles to the north. (J.Suter coll.)

EDALE

XI. The village and its station are near the left border of this 1947 map, which is scaled at 2ins to 1 mile. Below them is the severely curved A625, which made transport history when it kept slipping down the side of Mam Tor and had to be closed in 1979. It had been built in 1819 on shale on sloping sandstone. A straight but inclined road was built soon after. Blue John Mine is shown nearby. It still produces a rare and unique luxury gemstone, known as fluorspar. Hope is on the right of the page, but its station is just on the next one. Bamford village and station are a further mile on. Above them is the Derwent Valley Board's Aqueduct. The six mile-long River Derwent ends at the Ladybower Reservoir dam. Extending north can be seen part of the three very extensive reservoirs built in 1902-16 to serve the Sheffield district and much of the North Midlands. Further major structures were built in 1935-43. To aid the provision of materials and equipment, a long siding was laid north in the Bamford area.

Bents

Dovestone Brook

Salt Cellar

Old Ho.

White Tor 1599

High Ho.

Grindle Barn

Raddlepit Rushes

Derwent Moors

Derwent Edge

Wheel Stones

Shooting Cabin   Moscar Ho.

Striding Edge

Rising Clough

bridge end Pasture

Lee Wood

Grainfoot Fm

DERWENT   Hurkling Stones

ead Cote

280

Riding Ho.

Lodge Cote

Whinstone Lee Tor

Cutthroat Br.

Highshaw Clough

rm Fields

ybower Reservoir

Derwent Valley Wr Bd

Crookhill Fm

Crookhill Hill

Ladybower Tor 1198

Ladybower Inn

Ladybower Ho.

10

Priddock Wood

Ladybower Brook

Hordron Edge

Moscar Fields

Stone Circle

142

Stanage End

ther shop

yclough

Ashop Fm

Jarvis Clough

Moscar Moor

Crow Chin

1241

Shooting Cabin

250

Bamford Edge

Bamford Moor

Thornhill Brink

Win Hill 1523

Yorkshire Br.

250

Inn

Great Tor

Tumuli

1395

250

Twitchill Fm

A

Edge Green Dimings

Highfield Head

Derwent Valley Water Bd

Aqueduct Bridge

K

Bole Hill

Aston

Thornhill

Hallam Barn

Carr Inn Bottom

Bamford

Upper Hurst

Camp Mill

Inn 513

Weir Mills (Cotton)

Bamford Filters

Rec.

Upper Hurst Br.

Nether Hurst

h Ho.

R. Noe   Shatton

Brough

Inn

A.625

Golf Course

Shawhay Barn

Cunliffe

750

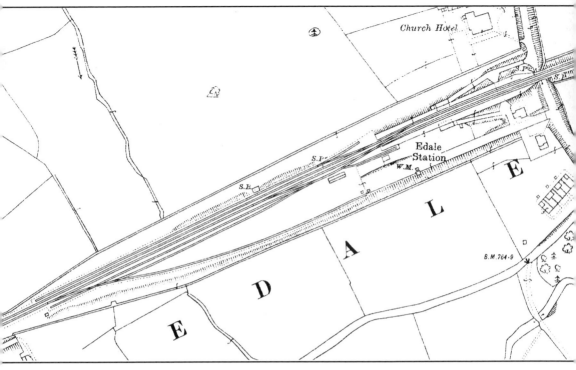

XII. The 1921 issue is scaled at 20ins to 1 mile and has sidings for local agricultural and domestic traffic. The population was 365 in 1901 and 361 in 1961.

39. An early postcard has the hotel beyond the platform fencing, with railway property on the left. The district was popular with walkers and a Youth Hostel was created later. (P.Laming coll.)

40. This late 1960s record shows the only way to pass between platforms. The map reveals that this bridge is to the west of the one in the previous view. Modern lighting has arrived. (R.S.Carpenter coll.)

41. A train of coal empties was recorded eastbound on 3rd October 1959, behind ex-WD 2-8-0 no. 90055. Their classification referred to the War Department, who had them built for use widely in the world during World War II. (M.J.Stretton coll.)

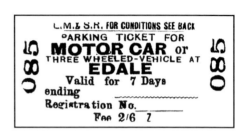

L.M.& S.R. FOR CONDITIONS SEE BACK
PARKING TICKET FOR
085 **MOTOR CAR** or 085
THREE WHEELED-VEHICLE AT
EDALE
Valid for 7 Days
ending ⌒⌒⌒⌒⌒⌒
Registration No._____
Fee 2/6 Z

← 42. Class 4MT 2-6-4T no. 42379 waits with its special train on 30th September 1961. The splendidly situated hotel on the left was still open to enjoy the views, but it was later renamed 'The Rambler'. The station became unstaffed on 7th September 1969. (Colour-Rail.com)

↙ 43. A 1964 panorama includes the structures provided when the station opened on 25th June 1894, like the others in the Hope Valley. Only the details had been modernised. (Stations UK)

↓ 44. The signal box came into use with 20 levers on 29th October 1893 and they were still in use in 2020. Passing on 8th August 1986 is DMU no. 142006 working the 15.45 Sheffield to Manchester. One siding remains for the use of the engineers. The goods yard had closed on 7th October 1963. (M.P.Turvey)

45. Westbound on 9th June 2004 is no. 60081 with a train of hoppers used for mineral traffic. Sadly many of the lineside views had been lost by tree overgrowth. The engine carries a brass nameplate showing *Isambard Kingdom Brunel*. (R.J.Stewart-Smith)

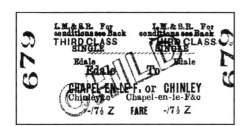

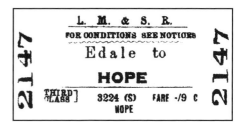

46. It is 27th April 2005 and no. 66547 passes with the 09.58 Tunstead-West Burton Power Station limestone haul. We see the matching stone-built waiting shelters and the signal box in the background. The Pennine Way now starts here for the joy of those with mobility of a suitable type. (A.C.Hartless)

47. Seen on the same day, Pacer no. 142014 departs with the 10.14 Sheffield-Manchester Piccadilly. Note the two semaphore signals beyond the station. By 2017-18, over 89,000 tickets were issued annually here. (A.C.Hartless)

EAST OF EDALE
Normans Bank

48.   This box opened in 1906 with six levers and lasted until 24th April 1960. Seen in 1955, it then had eight levers, but four were spare! The site was named after Normans Farm, which can be found on map XI. (R.S.Carpenter coll.)

WEST OF HOPE

Earle's Sidings

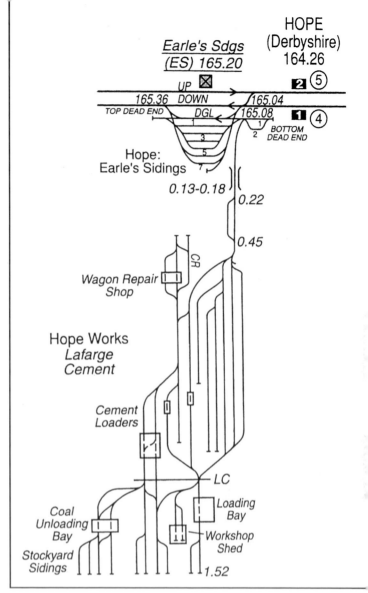

XIII. This 2013 diagram has the number of coaches to suit each platform in circles. 'LC' indicates a level crossing. The line passes over the A625 on a bridge, which is now just east of Hope College. It is a concrete one, with fine ornamentation. (©TRACKmaps)

↓ 49. Part of the extensive exchange sidings was recorded on 27th June 1972 as a DMU runs past. The facilities were soon to be greatly extended as the cement output was increasingly moved by rail from the Peak District National Park. This was formed in 1951 and its action moved minerals from road to rail. The first firm to own the works was G&T Earle Ltd. (J.Suter coll.)

50. No. 45126 passes Earle's Sidings with the twice-weekly 10.27 Halewood-Tinsley scrap metal train on 28th August 1986. It comprised vacuum-braked tippler and mineral wagons, which were quite a rarity by that time. The exchange sidings for Blue Circle hold three different wagon types: air-braked tanks on the left, vacuum-braked Presflos in the middle and vacuum-braked Cemflos on the right. The 1½ mile long branch south to the cement works is visible in the left foreground. Included is the 35-lever signal box, which was opened on 14th April 1929 and was rebuilt after a fire in about 1975. (P.D.Shannon)

51.   Seen on the same day, no. 47103 sets out from the west end of Earle's Sidings with the 19.50 departure to Northenden. The train comprises vacuum-braked Presflo wagons, which by this time were used only on flows to Northenden and Melton. (P.D.Shannon)

Hope Cement Works

52.   Running south through the countryside west of Hope in May 1943 is the works' 0-6-0T *Nunlow*. The firm's pride was built by Hudswell Clarke in 1938. It was named after a nearby hill called Nun Low. The engine is now preserved by the Bahamas Locomotive Society, and moved to the Dinting Railway Centre near Glossop in 1968. Following its closure in 1990, *Nunlow* spent the summer on loan to the Swanage Railway in Dorset. It then moved to the Society's new home on the Keighley & Worth Valley Railway where, following the completion of the Society's museum at Ingrow in May 2003, it became one of the major exhibits. (R.S.Carpenter coll.)

53.   The firm had extensive maintenance facilities and, here, its 0-4-0ST *Pindale* is being serviced on 19th November 1955. It was used to bring in 350-ton trains of coal, gypsum and other goods, and take out 21 vans of bagged cement. About 10 trains a day were run to and from the exchange sidings. It was named after a nearby quarry and was built in about 1928 by George Inglis & Co, at Albert Works in Airdrie. (R.Humm coll.)

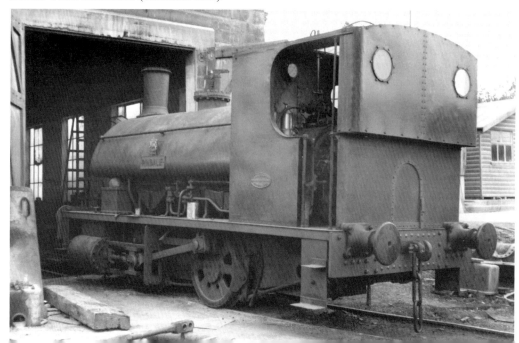

54. In the 1960s, the works became part of the Blue Circle Group and underwent a major reconstruction and capacity increase. In 2001, Blue Circle became part of the international Lafarge Group. In 2012, Lafarge merged their UK construction materials business with that of Tarmac. Here we see English Electric Bo-Bo loco nos 20905 and 20906 on 16th September 2005. They ran to Crewe for fuel and examination every 72 hours. (R.J.Stewart-Smith)

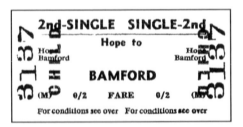

55. At work on 30th June 2010 is the firm's Hunslet Barclay with works no. 773 of 1989. It is carrying the local name of *Blue John* and is close to a shunt signal. Coal inwards was being reduced by the use of car tyres and deceased animal parts for burning. (A.J.Booth)

56. We move forward to 21st June 2011 and see another EE Bo-Bo. This time it is in its new owner's colours, but still carries its original number, no. 20168. A brass nameplate is carried on its frame bearing the name of *Sir George Earle*, a founder of the works. The Breedon Group took over the production in 2016. (A.J.Booth)

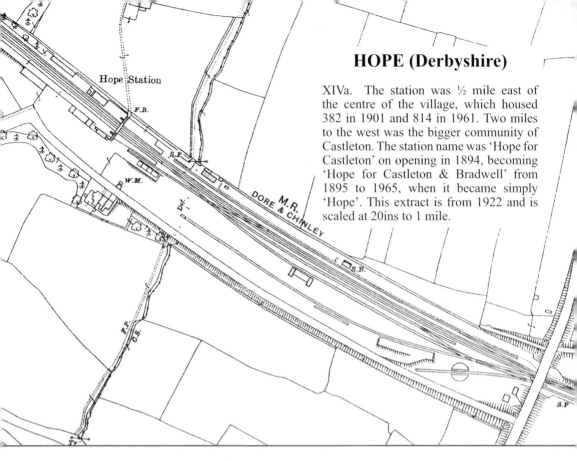

HOPE (Derbyshire)

XIVa. The station was ½ mile east of the centre of the village, which housed 382 in 1901 and 814 in 1961. Two miles to the west was the bigger community of Castleton. The station name was 'Hope for Castleton' on opening in 1894, becoming 'Hope for Castleton & Bradwell' from 1895 to 1965, when it became simply 'Hope'. This extract is from 1922 and is scaled at 20ins to 1 mile.

57. The toilet signs are closest in this view westwards from the footbridge in 1904. Only three doors are open as this troop of 1st Volunteer Battalion Northumberland Fusiliers awaits orders. It has probably been on an exercise in the Peaks. The soldiers are wearing slouch hats, which were still worn on manoeuvres as late as 1905; the left side of the brim was turned up to allow a rifle to be slung over the shoulder. (J.Alsop coll.)

58.   An early survey eastwards contains part of the goods yard and includes the station master, under a bowler hat, the porter, with brass buttons, and some gentlemen. Ladies were kept in the distance. (J.Alsop coll.)

59.   The footbridge was the ideal location to record the fine panorama that the High Peak presents westwards. Beyond Kinder Scout and Edale Moor is Hayfield, hidden in the Sett Valley. (J.Alsop coll.)

60. The station is in the distance, beyond the signal box which had 21 levers and remained in use until 5th August 1964. The extensive goods yard had closed on 20th April of that year. Only one 2-ton crane was provided, plus a loading dock. (Bentley coll.)

61. Seen on 23rd August 1958 is no. 44267, a class 4F 0-6-0. Station staffing ceased on 7th September 1969 and destruction of the 1894 structures followed, eventually. This popular 0-6-0 design was introduced by the MR in 1911. (J.Suter coll.)

62.   The suffix 'Derbyshire' was used by BR in 1979-87, and again later. There is also a 'Hope' in Flintshire. There is grass extensively on 4th August 1986 as no. 31431 runs under the original footbridge with the 17.45 Liverpool to Hull service. The locomotive's sector was Provincial General. (M.P.Turvey)

63.   Midland Main Line High Speed Train no. 43195 *Rio Swift* is seen on 9th September 2004, while working the 15.47 Manchester Piccadilly to St Pancras service. The brick huts would not stand for much longer, as shown by the next picture. (R.J.Stewart-Smith)

64. Annual passenger figures rose from around 54,000 in 2013 to 67,000 by 2017. An automatic ticket machine arrived in 2018 to relieve the guards' tasks. Pacer no. 142062 runs in on 25th June 2013 with the 14.45 Manchester to Sheffield service and the ramblers wait to select one of its small doorways. Most of this type of unit had gone by 2020. (A.C.Hartless)

EAST OF HOPE

XIVb. During construction of the Derwent and Howden dams between 1912 and 1916, a standard gauge railway branch carried stone from a quarry near Grindleford up to the worksite. This line was removed when the dams were completed, but reinstated during construction of the Ladybower Reservoir in 1935-43. A halt was built here in 1935, but never used. The reservoir was officially opened by King George VI on 24th September 1945. Shown is the MR trackwork in 1919, with the contractor's groundwork. Access to the old trackbed is on the Thornhill Trail. The signal box was relocated to Peak Rail. The box was open from 16th February 1902 to 8th April 1919 and again from 2nd December 1935 until 16th October 1949.

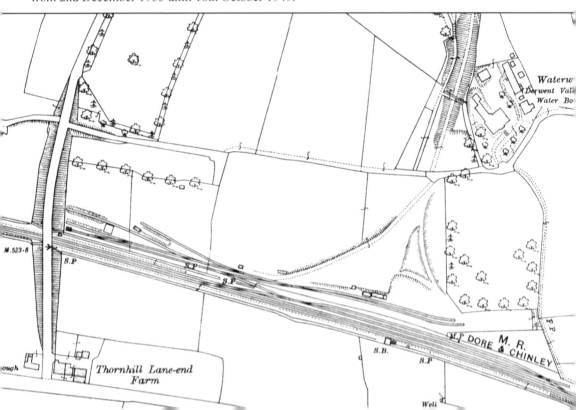

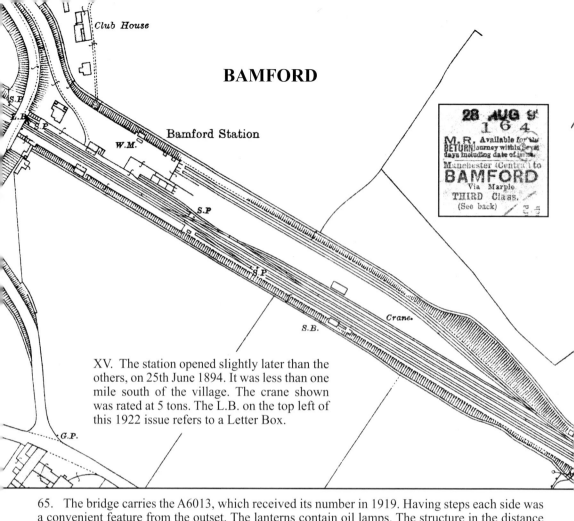

BAMFORD

Club House

Bamford Station

W.M.

S.P.

S.P.

S.B.

Crane.

G.P.

XV. The station opened slightly later than the others, on 25th June 1894. It was less than one mile south of the village. The crane shown was rated at 5 tons. The L.B. on the top left of this 1922 issue refers to a Letter Box.

65.   The bridge carries the A6013, which received its number in 1919. Having steps each side was a convenient feature from the outset. The lanterns contain oil lamps. The structure in the distance is part of the bridge over the River Derwent. (J.Alsop coll.)

66.   The gates to the platforms are on the left. The steps are in the last picture and on the map, as is the booking office. (J.Alsop coll.)

67.   We can enjoy a sunlit day in the 1950s. No. 43254 is working freight from Sheffield to Buxton. It is a class 3F 0-6-0, a type created by the MR in 1888. The small building on the left is the office for the weighing machine and the white one on the right is a grain store. (Bentley coll.)

68.   Closure of the passenger booking office came in 1969 and the last station master bought the house he had occupied. The other buildings were soon demolished. This panorama is from 11th July 1967. This was one of the last routes to have poles and overhead wires. (J.Suter coll.)

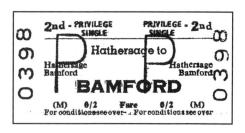

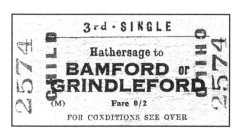

69. The 1.27pm New Mills to Sheffield was formed of a class 114 DMU 'Derby Heavyweight' on 19th March 1977. The village had once been noted for a big cotton mill and also a corn mill, which succeeded it. It changed from water power to steam, with a beam engine, but closed in the 1990s. (M.J.Stretton coll.)

70. The famous 4-6-2 no. 4472 *Flying Scotsman* is rushing through with a special train from Spalding to Blackburn on 24th November 1984. The goods yard had closed on 31st January 1966, but a new use had been found for its buildings. (T.Heavyside)

71. The signal box opened with the line on 29th October 1893 and was fitted with a 20-lever frame initially. After closure on 10th September 1989, the box was moved to Peak Rail for re-use (see our *Cromford & High Peak* album). Passing on 9th August 1986 is the 11.27 Sheffield to Manchester. It is formed of no. 142014, a 'Pacer' with two Leyland-style bus bodies each fitted with 62 seats and four wheels. (M.P.Turvey)

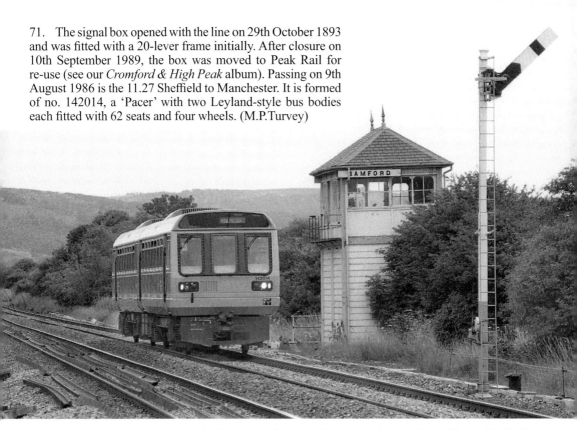

72. No. 150120 calls at Bamford with a stopping train from Manchester Piccadilly to Sheffield on 25th June 2018. The station had become an unstaffed halt in September 1969 when BR introduced a Paytrain service on the Hope Valley line. The village population increased from 510 in 1901 to 1097 in 1961. By 2020, it had the enterprise to create a community pub called *The Anglers Rest*. (P.D.Shannon)

HATHERSAGE

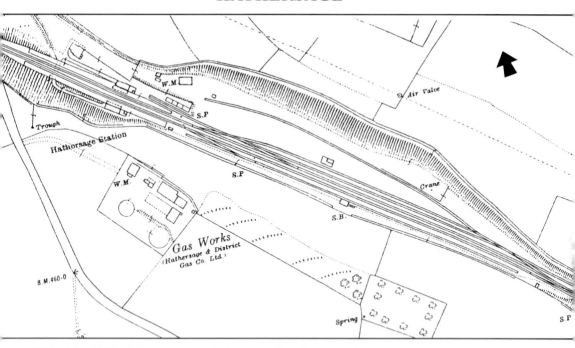

XVIa. The 1922 edition appears at 20ins to 1 mile. The crane shown was rated at 10 tons. The road running under the line was the A622. The village begins just north of the bridge. The gas works was a latecomer, being started in 1906, but it grew rapidly as surrounding villages were connected. Coal carbonised was about 2060 tons per annum by 1914 and had grown to 3700 tons (about 340 wagon loads) when a high-pressure main from Sheffield allowed production at Hathersage to cease in 1952. The Derwent Aqueduct runs diagonally, with dashes and an Air Valve.

73. This early view is from the north and has the entrance to the goods yard and the loading dock on the left. Modern kerbed footpaths were provided for those wishing to avoid the horse droppings, evident here. (J.Alsop coll.)

74. Hathersage was once an important centre for the manufacture of millstones, needles and pins. There are some outstanding areas of natural beauty surrounding the village, including Stanage and Burbage Edges. In the distance is the signal box, which had 24 levers and lasted until 19th November 1967. (P.Laming coll.)

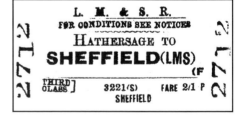

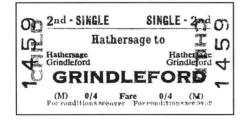

75.   This is the scene not long before staffing ceased on 7th September 1969. The road on the left was not used for goods traffic after 31st January 1965. The local population grew from 1135 in 1901 to 1522 in 1961. (J.Suter coll.)

76.   A 1964 view west reveals an important staff task: plant tub management. Floor boarding was used here to reduce platform weight on the embankment. The trailing point gave access to the yard for trains from the Sheffield direction. They reversed over it. (Stations UK)

EASTER RAIL CRUISE IN DERBYSHIRE

CHEAP TRIP

B Y

DIESEL TRAIN

HATHERSAGE

Sunday 14th April 1963

FROM	TIMES OF DEPARTURE	RETURN FARES Second Class	ARRIVAL TIMES ON RETURN
	pm	s d	pm
NOTTINGHAM Midland ...	2 30	8/3	8 43
BEESTON...	2 38		8 34
TRENT	2 45		8 24
SAWLEY JUNCTION ...	2 50		8 18
DRAYCOTT & BREASTON ...	2 55	7/6	8 14
BORROWASH	3 1		8 8
SPONDON	3 5		8 4
DERBY Midland	3 15	7/3	7 55
BELPER	3 29	5/6	7 43
AMBERGATE	3 35	5/3	7 36
	pm	Passengers return	pm
HATHERSAGE ... ... arrive	5 20	same day at ...	6 55

The train will proceed on the outward journey through the beautiful Derbyshire dales via Matlock, Bakewell and Miller's Dale and thence through the Hope Valley to Hathersage allowing approximately 1¼ hours' stay at that point. The return journey will be made via Grindleford, Chesterfield and Wingfield.

Children under 3 years of age, free; 3 years and under 14, half-fares (fractions of a 1d. reckoned as a 1d.).

Rail tickets can be obtained in advance at stations and official railway agents

Further information will be supplied on application to stations, official railway agents, or to Commercial Manager, Alan House, Clumber Street, Nottingham. Telephone 48531, Extn. 40.

Travel in Rail Comfort   March 1963   BR 35000

Arthur Grant & Sons (Printers) Ltd., Heanor, Derbyshire

XVIb.   Declining passenger numbers in the 1960s resulted in some enterprise being shown by BR officers.

77. Two-car class 142 numbered 142038 arrives on 12th October 1988, bound for Sheffield. Passenger numbers were in the range of 60,000 to 65,000 in 2013-18. The train will have just passed over Hathersage Viaduct. (Colour-Rail.com)

78. It is 27th September 2005 and the 08.52 Liverpool-Norwich speeds past, formed of DMU no. 170102, and giving us a view of the simple upside shelter. Step-free access is available to both platforms, which are linked via a ramped elderly subway. (A.C.Hartless)

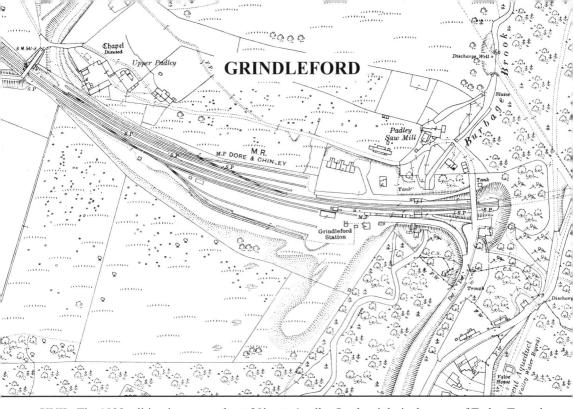

XVII. The 1922 edition is seen at about 20ins to 1 mile. On the right is the start of Totley Tunnel, which is 3 miles 950yds long and the second longest in the UK. It had five shafts up to Totley Moor, which is over 1200ft above sea level.

79. An early record includes both inclined access paths and the arched bridge, which carries a local road. The nearest village is Nether Padley, which is about a mile to the south. (J.Alsop coll.)

80.   We are at the road junction lower right on the map, looking north. The gate is over the road down to the station and the goods yard. The main building is centre here and on the right of the previous picture. (P.Laming coll.)

81.   About to enter Totley Tunnel in 1955 is no. 47997, a Beyer-Garratt 2-6-6-2T. It was one of 33 produced by the LMS in 1927-30 for heavy freight work. The crew members often tied rags over their faces for tunnel trips, such as this. (M.J.Stretton coll.)

82. Running towards the tunnel on 17th March 1962 is class 4F 0-6-0 no. 44053. To the left of the rear of the train are wagons in the goods yard and to the left of the WAY OUT pole is the top of the signal box. (R.Humm coll.)

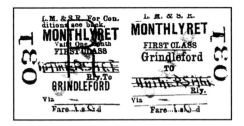

83.   A fine panorama from the bridge in 1964 includes the spacious goods shed. The yard closed soon after; it had the benefit of a 4-ton crane on offer. The platforms were later shortened to take just three cars each. (Stations UK)

84.   Station staffing ceased on 7th September 1969 and a new use for the main building was soon found. It is seen on 5th June 1971 and was still supplying nutrients and pleasure in 2020. The good menu is visible. (J.Langford)

85. No. 47331 passes Grindleford box with a loaded cement train from Earle's Sidings comprising air-braked tanks on 26th March 1981. The sidings in the foreground belong to the former station goods yard, which was still used for occasional wagon stabling in the 1980s. (P.D.Shannon)

86. It is 27th September 2005 and Express Sprinter unit no. 158972 leaves Totley Tunnel and runs through the station with the 09.30 Cleethorpes-Manchester Airport service. The tunnel took six years to build. Passenger usage here was over 60,000 in both 2017 and 2018. (A.C.Hartless)

➔ 87. No. 66613 emerges into daylight at the west end of Totley Tunnel on the same day, with the 09.53 Dewsbury-Earle's Sidings empty cement tanks. Note the plaque above the tunnel entrance; close inspection shows the date to be 1893 and not 1993 as it may first appear. (A.C.Hartless)

88. There had been another crossover in front of the signal box for many years. This is the second box and its 25-lever frame came into use on 20th November 1938. The structure is seen on 27th July 1985 and it and the siding were both still usable in 2013. (R.J.Stewart-Smith)

DORE & TOTLEY

➜ XVIII. The 1923 edition has the River Sheaf flowing from the lower to top border and the county boundary in its upper part. To the left of the railway is the A621, which runs north to Sheffield. The first station was on the MR main line and opened on 1st February 1870 as Dore & Totley (both are lower right). The suffix '& TOTLEY' was not used between March 1971 and 2nd April 2008. The two tracks on the right were added in 1902.

➜ *Inset:* The 1in to 1 mile map of 1947 has the east end of Totley Tunnel on its left border and the 1870 route on the right, curving south into Bradway Tunnel from the triangular junction. Its southern part is known as Dore South Curve and runs through a 91yd-long tunnel. The curve from west to south has seen little passenger traffic. One novel exception was between May 2003 and September 2004, when Midland Mainline operated an hourly service between London St Pancras and Manchester Piccadilly. 'Project Rio' provided direct services between the two cities, while the modernisation of the West Coast Main Line closed that route for lengthy periods.

B.M.387·7

Sheffield 4
Bakewell 12   M.8

Mill Race

B.Ps

Def.

S.Ps

Weirs

Weir

C.R.

F.B.   Limb Bridge   Dore Station
                            Junction
                            C.S.

B.P.   S.B.

Weir

C.R.

S.Ps

ABBEYDALE ROAD

B.M.393·4

F.B.

Dore & Totley
Station

L.B.

Def.

G.P.

S.P   S.P   O.C.   P.W.

The Moss   Abbeydale

Moorbottom Fm
Ryecroft

Inn   L.B.

Smithy

Abbeydale Park

Ch.
Dore   Brinkburn
          Grange

Totley
Brook

ABBEYDALE STA

Ch.

Totley
Rise

Cherrytree
Orphanage

Totley   S. Georges Fm
Inn   Smithy

89. This is thought to be an original MR photograph. We are looking north, when there were only two tracks and platforms, which means prior to 1902. In the foreground was the barrow crossing and in the background is the new signal box. (R.S.Carpenter coll.)

90. Following the quadrupling, the far platform was widened and received a new building with a long canopy, as seen here. The small building in line with it is probably the station's coal shed. (J.Alsop coll.)

91. This is the view from from Twentywell Lane overbridge. Signals were not always placed adjacent to the track they served, but in the best viewing position. The last map shows the posts (S.P.), but the box is beyond the lower border. (J.Alsop coll.)

92. This is another view from Twentywell Lane, and is dated 21st May 1956. The platforms have been extended and the signal has been removed. Class 4F 0-6-0 no. 43854 is bound for New Mills. A new 48-lever box came into use on 20th October 1901 and it received a panel on 16th January 1972, but this worked only to 25th March 1973. (J.Suter coll.)

93. On the left is the main line south to Chesterfield and on the right are the tracks from the Hope Valley and New Mills. The board on the right carries pulley wheels for signal wires and these are protected by the other wooden panels. (R.S.Carpenter coll.)

94. No. 47446 passes through with a special for Manchester via the Hope Valley comprising air-conditioned stock, on 5th July 1983. The Manchester line through Dore was singled in 1985, creating a serious bottleneck as the frequency of passenger trains increased. (P.D.Shannon)

2nd- SPECIAL   SPECIAL -2nd
CHEAP SINGLE   CHEAP SINGLE

Dore & Totley to

Dore & Totley   Dore & Totley
Millhouses &   Millhouses &
Ecclesall   Ecclesall

MILLHOUSES & ECCLESALL

(E)   (E)
For conditions see over   For conditions see over

0026   0026

L. M. & S. R.

Issued subject to the conditions & regulations
the Coy Time Tables Books Bills & Notices and in
the Railway Coy Book of regulations relating to
traffic by Passenger train or other similar service

CHEAP SINGLE TICKET
Dore & Totley to
SHEFFIELD (LMS)

FIRST CLASS]   3219 (CST   FARE ·/5
        SHEFFIELD

563

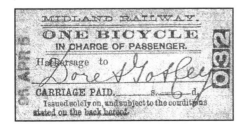

MIDLAND RAILWAY.

ONE BICYCLE
IN CHARGE OF PASSENGER.

Harborage to *Dore & Totley*

CARRIAGE PAID.   s.   d.

Issued solely on, and subject to the conditions
stated on the back hereof.

05 APR 5   082

🚂 **Charter control**   2nd

Totley County School

Tuesday, 8th July, 1986

Dore

to

Cleethorpes and back

For conditions see over (E)

0195   0195

95.   It is 27th September 2005 and the west side of the main building shows the prospective diner's perspective. A canopy was added on the other side, over the platform, in May 2019, when the restaurant was still busy. (A.C.Hartless)

96.   The station became unstaffed in 1969 and the Chesterfield platforms were removed later. This is the scene on 16th February 2013 and no. 158774 was recorded on the left. A 129-space car park was created that year. (A.F.Bullimore)

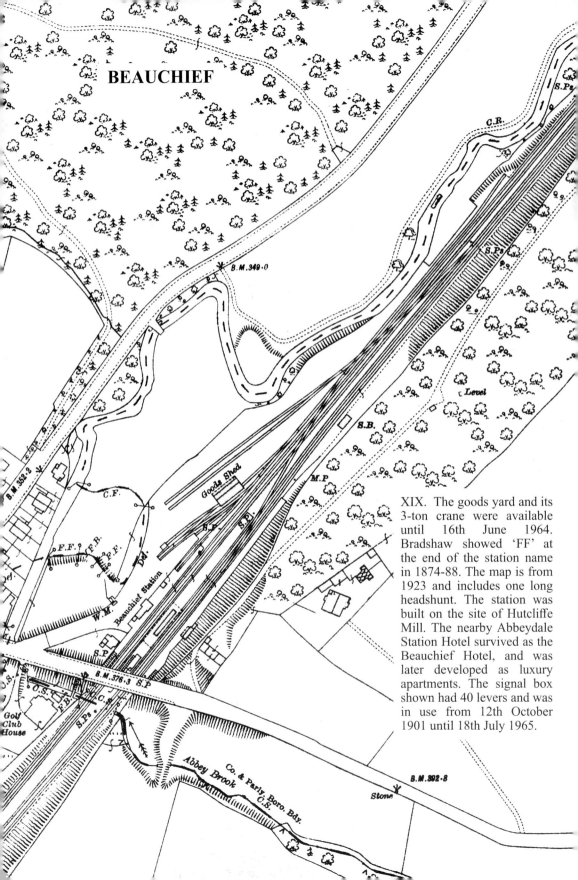

BEAUCHIEF

B.M. 349·0

C.R.

S.Ps.

S.Ps.

Level

S.B.

M.P

Goods Shed

S.P.

S.P.

S.P.

C.F.

Dd.

F.F.

F.B.

F.F.

W.M.

Beauchief Station

S.P.

B.M. 352·2

B.M. 376·3 S.P.

O.S.

O.S.

F.B.

S.C.

S.Ps.

Golf
Club
House

Abbey Brook

Co. & Parly. Boro. Bdy.
C.S.

B.M. 392·8

Stone

XIX. The goods yard and its
3-ton crane were available
until 16th June 1964.
Bradshaw showed 'FF' at
the end of the station name
in 1874-88. The map is from
1923 and includes one long
headshunt. The station was
built on the site of Hutcliffe
Mill. The nearby Abbeydale
Station Hotel survived as the
Beauchief Hotel, and was
later developed as luxury
apartments. The signal box
shown had 40 levers and was
in use from 12th October
1901 until 18th July 1965.

97. The station name was pronounced *Beechif*. On 1st February 1870 it opened as Abbey Houses, but on 1st April of the same year it was renamed Beauchieff. It was renamed again on 1st June 1874 as Beauchieff & Abbey Dale, becoming Beauchief & Abbey Dale on 1st October 1888. (J.Alsop coll.)

98. In 1901-03 the station was expanded to four platforms and on 19th March 1914 it was renamed Beauchief. On 2nd January 1961, it closed to passengers and goods yard closure followed on 16th June 1964. This is an MR 2-4-0 built in the 1870s, when their classifications were changing. This appears to be an 890 class. (Bentley coll.)

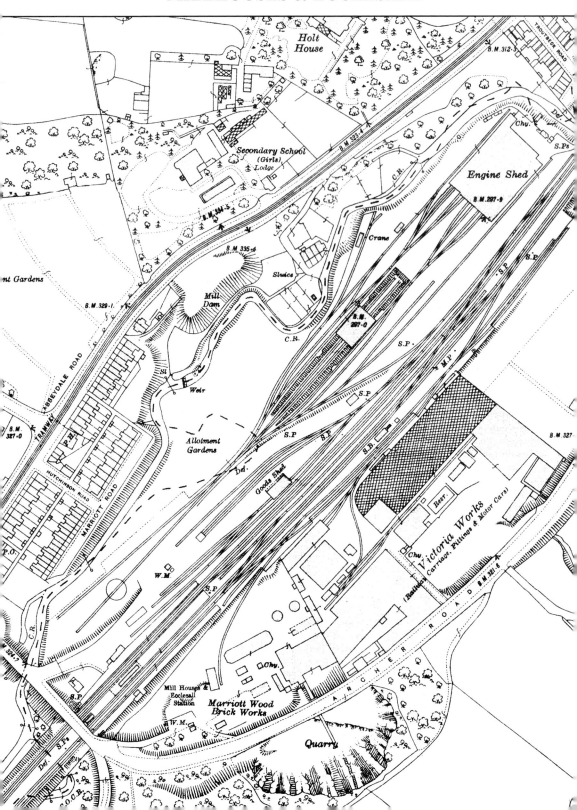

← XX. The 1920 edition has the station lower left and Sheffield Millhouses Engine Shed top right. It was MR property then and can be seen in pictures 103 and 104. Part of the Sheffield Tramway is diagonally top left, along Abbeydale Road. The works lower right are worthy of study. The large signal box near Victoria Works had 52 levers and was worked from 12th January 1902 to 21st January 1973.

99. On 1st February 1870 the station opened as Ecclesall, and on 1st October 1871 it was renamed Ecclesall & Mill Houses. It was renamed again on 1st May 1884 as Mill Houses & Ecclesall. In 1901-03 it was expanded to four platforms. Finally, on 18th July 1932 it was renamed Millhouses & Ecclesall for the last time. (J.Suter coll.)

100. Running in on the line from New Mills in July 1963 is class 5MT 4-6-0 no. 45139. This view includes the steps down from the road, plus the roof over the station offices. (Colour-Rail.com)

101. This panorama from July 1967 includes the spacious facilities provided for passengers in 1903. They were all to be closed on 10th June 1968. The goods yard was in use until 24th April 1972. (J.Suter coll.)

102. It is 1st September 1972 and we witness an up passenger train from the top of the closed steps. Most of the buildings disappeared in the 1980s, but the home once used by the station master remained as a dwelling. Agriculture and industries of this area have largely gone, thus the area is now mainly residential. Millhouses was once a small hamlet, which grew around Ecclesall Corn Mill. (T.Heavyside)

Millhouses Engine Shed

103. The MR building had eight roads and was adjacent to the River Sheaf, which was a convenient source of boiler water. The shed was opened in 1901 and coded 19B in 1948-58 and 41C in 1958-62. (J.Suter coll.)

104. Centre stage are class 2MT 2-6-0 no. 46494 and 4-4-0 no. 40537. Much maintenance work had been undertaken here earlier. The allocation was 41 in 1950 and 33 in 1959. Closure came on 1st January 1962. (Colour-Rail.com)

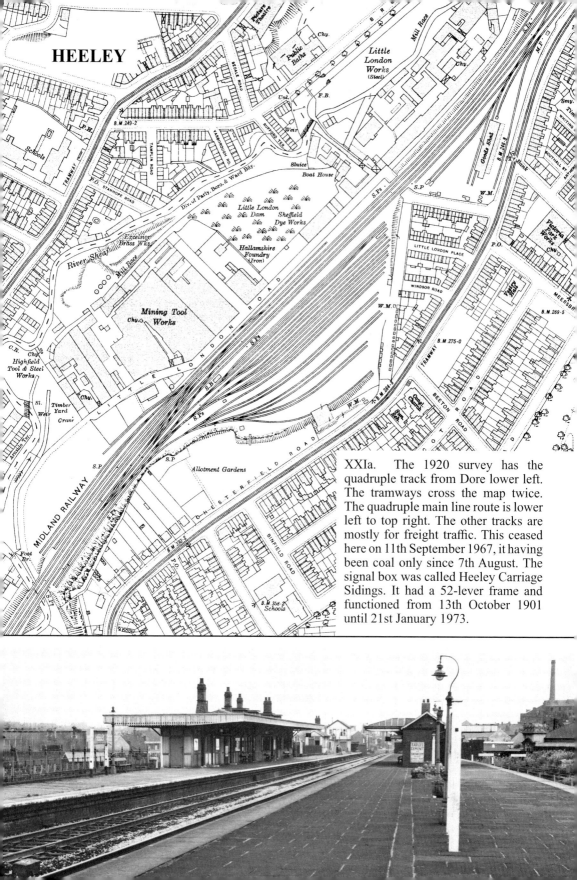

HEELEY

XXIa. The 1920 survey has the quadruple track from Dore lower left. The tramways cross the map twice. The quadruple main line route is lower left to top right. The other tracks are mostly for freight traffic. This ceased here on 11th September 1967, it having been coal only since 7th August. The signal box was called Heeley Carriage Sidings. It had a 52-lever frame and functioned from 13th October 1901 until 21st January 1973.

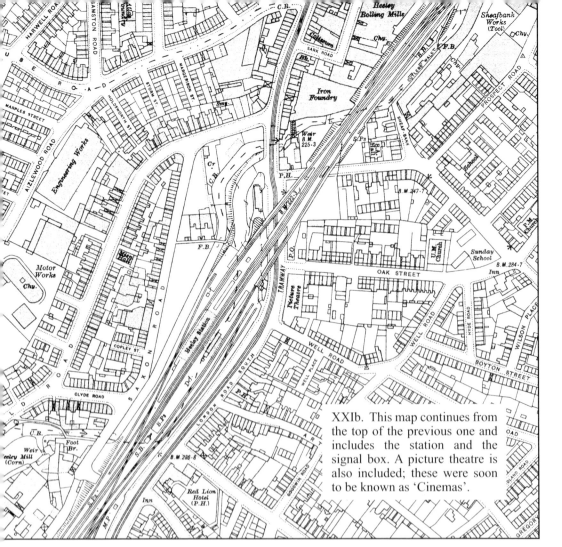

XXIb. This map continues from the top of the previous one and includes the station and the signal box. A picture theatre is also included; these were soon to be known as 'Cinemas'.

↙ 105. This view is from 8th July 1967 and it includes the signal box. The station was open from 1st February 1870 to 10th June 1968. It was built on an embankment between the A61, London Road South and the River Sheaf. During construction, both the road and river were diverted to create space for the station and sidings. (J.Suter coll.)

→ 106. We are looking north on 23rd January 1967 at the third box to have been built here. It was in use from 18th October 1931 to 7th January 1973. Heeley North Junction box was open from 4th May 1902 until 18th October 1931. (R.Humm coll.)

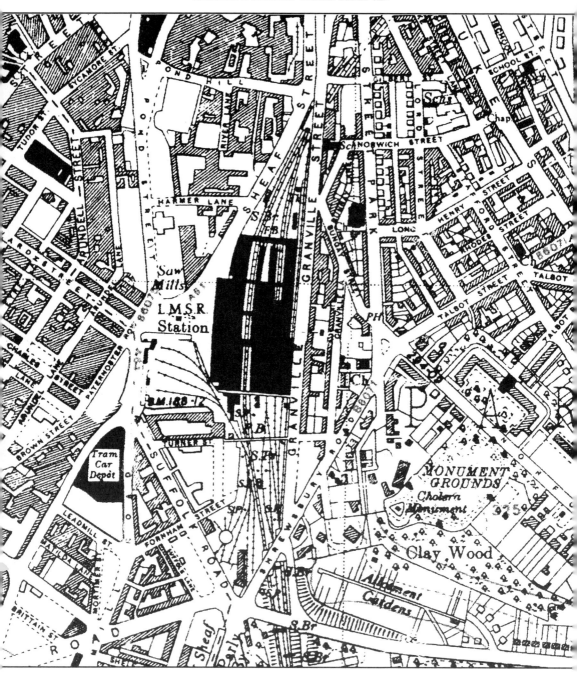

XXII. We arrive over the lower border of this 1948 map, shown at 12ins to 1 mile. The route continues at the top into Broad Street Tunnel. A tram depot is shown. The first tramway operated until October 1960; the tram tracks are on the next map. The station name was 'Sheffield New Midland' until 1st February 1876. The suffix 'Midland' was then applied until 25th September 1950. Subsequently 'City' was used until 18th June 1951 when it reverted to 'Sheffield Midland'. It became plain 'Sheffield' on 4th May 1970, following the closure of Victoria on 5th January 1970.

107. The station and Pond Street Goods Depot opened on 1st February 1870, a damp and cold day, without any celebrations. There were originally different passenger entrances for each class of person. Their tickets were printed accordingly. (J.Suter coll.)

108. Uniformed porters await the arrival of 1st class passengers. The station was given two extra platforms and a new frontage in 1905. The enlargements consisted of creating an island platform out of the old platform 1 and building a new platform 1 and a new entrance. (R.Humm coll.)

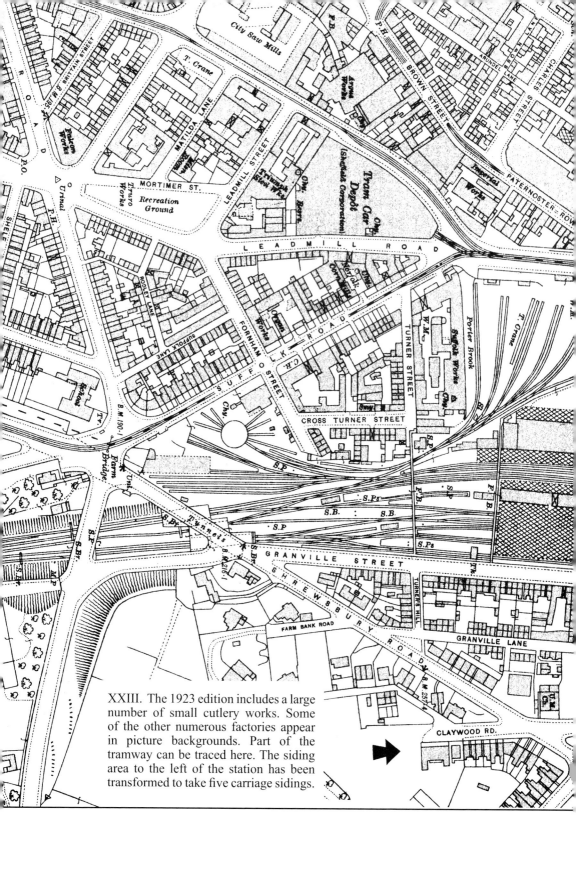

XXIII. The 1923 edition includes a large number of small cutlery works. Some of the other numerous factories appear in picture backgrounds. Part of the tramway can be traced here. The siding area to the left of the station has been transformed to take five carriage sidings.

109. The spacious result is revealed in this clear record. MR 2-4-0 no. 266 is waiting to depart northwards, its crew correctly avoiding smoke production in the station. (R.Humm coll.)

MIDLAND RAILWAY This Ticket is issued subject to the Regulations & Conditions stated in the Company's Time Tables & Bills.

FIRST CLASS.   FIRST CLASS.
AVAILABLE ON DAY OF ISSUE ONLY

BEAUCHIEF to

SHEFFIELD

FARE 6d.   FARE 6d.

Beauchief-Sheffield   Beauchief Sheffield

2nd - SPECIAL   SPECIAL - 2nd
CHEAP SINGLE   CHEAP SINGLE

Millhouses & Ecclesall to
Millhouses &   Millhouses &
Ecclesall   Ecclesall
Sheffield   Sheffield
(Midland)   (Midland)

SHEFFIELD (MIDLAND)

(E)   (E)
For conditions see over   For conditions see over

BRITISH RAILWAYS (E)
FURLOUGH

FOR CONDITIONS SEE BACK. Available for three days, including day of issue.

MILLHOUSES & ECCLESALL to

Via

THIRD CLASS

2nd-SINGLE   SINGLE-2nd

Millhouses & Ecclesall to
Millhouses & Ecclesall   Millhouses & Ecclesall
Sheffield (Midland)   Sheffield (Midland)

SHEFFIELD (Midland)

(E)   0/   Fare   0/   (E)
For conditions see over   For conditions see over

110. The roof lost its glass during the bombing of World War II, but the metal frames were not removed until 1956. It is 29th July 1954 and class 2 2-6-0 no. 46493 is accelerating south with a train for Chinley. The coach is reflecting the platform edge. (R.Humm coll.)

111. Sheffield South No. 2 box is nearest and No. 1 Box is centre in this view from 24th October 1969. The latter had been rebuilt in 1940, following Nazi bombing. Closure came on 21st January 1973 for both boxes. (J.Suter coll.)

SHEFFIELD

↑ 112. No. 31126 runs in on 26th May 1979 hauling a train from Skegness. This type was built by Brush Traction in 1957-62 and they were fitted with English Electric 12 cylinder engines from 1964. The DMUs are waiting between trips. (T.Heavyside)

↗ 113. We can now enjoy three views from 19th July 1981; from the outside in. Two clocks were thoughtfully positioned outside. (D.A.Thompson)

→ 114. The original station buildings have been preserved and are between island platforms 2 to 5. There is now a 678-space car park situated next to the main building. (D.A.Thompson)

MIDLAND RAILWAY. This Ticket is issued subject to the Regulations & Conditions stated in the Company's Time Tables & Bills.
FIRST CLASS.   FIRST CLASS.
AVAILABLE ON DAY OF ISSUE ONLY
(A) SHEFFIELD to (A)
BEAUCHIEF
FARE 6d.   FARE 6d.
Sheffield-Beauchief   Sheffield-Beauchief

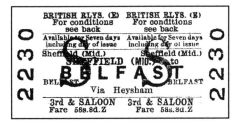

BRITISH RLYS. (E)   BRITISH RLYS. (E)
For conditions   For conditions
see back   see back
Available for Seven days   Available for Seven days
including day of issue   including day of issue
Sheffield (Mid.)   Sheffield (Mid.)
SHEFFIELD (MID.) to
BELFAST
BELFAST   BELFAST
Via Heysham
3rd & SALOON   3rd & SALOON
Fare 58s.8d.Z   Fare 58s.8d.Z

115. Two berthing sidings were still in use. There had been two crossovers for many decades in the steam era. They had been used to allow locomotives to run round their trains after arrival. (D.A.Thompson)

116. Now we witness no. 43029 on 26th May 1986 at the south end of platform 2. A new signal box with panels was opened at the south end of the platform on 21st January 1973 and was closed in 2015, the area coming under control of York. Above the second coach is a lift tower. The bridge for passengers and trolleys extends left of it. The two power cars each weighed 69 tons and had a maximum speed of 125mph. (M.P.Turvey)

↑ 117. Seen on the same day is a local service destined for Leeds and formed of class 114 two-car Derby Works products. Forty-nine were built and most coaches had 74 seats. They were made from 1956 and weighed 29 tons. (M.P.Turvey)

118. We are not back to the steam era, but watch the watering of a fine locomotive on 31st August 1991. It is no. 53809, a class 7F 2-8-0 introduced by the Somerset & Dorset Railway in 1914 and here showing its BR emblem of a Lion & Monocycle. It is on its way to an open day; the assisting diesel, no. 97201 *Experiment*, is dead, hence the brake van. In 2002, Midland Mainline started a major regeneration of the station. Prior to this, a taxi rank was located inside what is now the main concourse and the new entrance hall. The stone façade of the station was sandblasted and its archways filled with unobstructed windows to improve views both from inside and out. (R.J.Stewart-Smith)

↗ 119. The new Sheffield Supertrams called nearby from 22nd August 1994 and moved to a stop further south on 27th October 2002. We move on to 5th March 2013 to see bay platforms 3 and 4 at the north end of the station. DMU no. 150118 waits at the latter and we see the top of another lift shaft at this well-modernised station. (P.Jones)

→ 120. The south end of Sheffield station is pictured on 13th August 2014. On the right is Northern unit no. 158860, carrying a special livery promoting the Yorkshire town of Keighley. On the left is Northern Pacer no. 142027. The bridge above the platform ends carries a public footpath across the station. The platforms were generally used as follows: Platforms 1 and 2 - Northern to Huddersfield (via Barnsley and Penistone) and to Leeds via Barnsley (express); TransPennine Express to Cleethorpes; CrossCountry to Newcastle and Scotland, Platform 2C - Northern stopping trains to Manchester Piccadilly, Platforms 3 and 4 - local stopping trains to Leeds (both routes), Lincoln, Adwick and Scarborough/Bridlington/Hull, Platform 5 - East Midlands Railway to London, Norwich and Nottingham; CrossCountry to Birmingham, Reading and Exeter, Platform 6 - CrossCountry to Birmingham, Reading and Exeter, Northern to Nottingham (via Alfreton), TransPennine Express to Manchester Airport, Platform 7 - East Midlands Railway to Norwich and Liverpool, and Platform 8 - East Midlands Railway to Manchester and Liverpool; East Midlands Railway to London. (P.D.Shannon)

Other views of Sheffield's main stations can be found in Middleton Press albums, *Gainsborough to Sheffield* **and** *Sheffield towards Manchester.*

EVOLVING THE

ULTIMATE RAIL ENCYCLOPEDIA

INTERNATIONAL

Easebourne Midhurst GU29 9AZ. Tel:01730 813169

A-978 0 906520 B- 978 1 873793 C- 978 1 901706 D-978 1 904474
E - 978 1 906008 F - 978 1 908174 G - 978 1 910356

Our RAILWAY titles are listed below. Please check availability by looking at our website **www.middletonpress.co.uk**, telephoning us or by requesting a Brochure which includes our LATEST RAILWAY TITLES also our TRAMWAY, TROLLEYBUS, MILITARY and COASTAL series.

email:info@middletonpress.co.uk

A
Abergavenny to Merthyr C 91 8
Abertillery & Ebbw Vale Lines D 84 5
Aberystwyth to Carmarthen E 90 1
Allhallows - Branch Line to A 62 8
Alton - Branch Lines to A 11 6
Ambergate to Buxton G 28 9
Andover to Southampton A 82 6
Ascot - Branch Lines around A 64 2
Ashburton - Branch Line to B 95 4
Ashford - Steam to Eurostar B 67 1
Ashford to Dover A 48 2
Austrian Narrow Gauge D 04 3
Avonmouth - BL around D 42 5
Aylesbury to Rugby D 91 3
B
Baker Street to Uxbridge D 90 6
Bala to Llandudno E 87 1
Banbury to Birmingham D 27 2
Banbury to Cheltenham E 63 5
Bangor to Holyhead F 01 7
Bangor to Portmadoc E 72 7
Barking to Southend C 80 2
Barmouth to Pwllheli E 53 6
Barry - Branch Lines around D 50 0
Bartlow - Branch Lines to F 27 7
Basingstoke to Salisbury A 89 4
Bath Green Park to Bristol C 36 9
Bath to Evercreech Junction A 60 4
Beamish 40 years on rails E94 9
Bedford to Wellingborough D 31 9
Berwick to Drem F 64 2
Berwick to St. Boswells F 75 8
B'ham to Tamworth & Nuneaton F 63 5
Birkenhead to West Kirby F 61 1
Birmingham to Wolverhampton E253
Blackburn to Hellifield F 95 6
Bletchley to Cambridge D 94 4
Bletchley to Rugby E 07 9
Bodmin - Branch Lines around B 83 1
Boston to Lincoln F 80 2
Bournemouth to Evercreech Jn A 46 8
Bournemouth to Weymouth A 57 4
Bradshaw's History F18 5
Bradshaw's Rail Times 1850 F 13 0
Branch Lines series - see town names
Brecon to Neath D 43 2
Brecon to Newport D 16 6
Brecon to Newtown E 06 2
Brighton to Eastbourne A 16 1
Brighton to Worthing A 03 1
Bristol to Taunton D 03 6
Bromley South to Rochester B 23 7
Bromsgrove to Birmingham D 87 6
Bromsgrove to Gloucester D 73 9
Broxbourne to Cambridge F16 1
Brunel - A railtour D 74 6
Bude - Branch Line to B 29 9
Burnham to Evercreech Jn B 68 0
Buxton to Stockport G 32 6
C
Cambridge to Ely D 55 5
Canterbury - BLs around B 58 9
Cardiff to Dowlais (Cae Harris) E 47 5
Cardiff to Pontypridd E 95 6
Cardiff to Swansea E 42 0
Carlisle to Hawick E 85 7
Carmarthen to Fishguard E 66 6
Caterham & Tattenham Corner B251
Central & Southern Spain NG E 91 8
Chard and Yeovil - BLs a C 30 7
Charing Cross to Dartford A 75 8
Charing Cross to Orpington A 96 3
Cheddar - Branch Line to B 90 9
Cheltenham to Andover C 43 7
Cheltenham to Redditch D 81 4
Chesterfield to Lincoln G 21 0
Chester to Birkenhead F 21 5
Chester to Manchester F 51 2
Chester to Rhyl E 93 2
Chester to Warrington F 40 6
Chichester to Portsmouth A 14 7
Clacton and Walton - BLs to F 04 8
Clapham Jn to Beckenham Jn B 36 7
Cleobury Mortimer - BLs a E 18 5
Clevedon & Portishead - BLs to D180
Consett to South Shields E 57 4
Cornwall Narrow Gauge D 56 2
Corris and Vale of Rheidol E 65 9
Coventry to Leicester G 00 5
Craven Arms to Llandeilo E 35 2
Craven Arms to Wellington E 33 8
Crawley to Littlehampton A 34 5
Crewe to Manchester F 57 4
Crewe to Wigan G 12 8
Cromer - Branch Lines around C 26 0
Cromford and High Peak G 35 7
Croydon to East Grinstead B 48 0
Crystal Palace & Catford Loop B 87 1
Cyprus Narrow Gauge E 13 0
D
Darjeeling Revisited F 09 3
Darlington Leamside Newcastle E 28 4
Darlington to Newcastle D 98 2
Dartford to Sittingbourne B 34 3
Denbigh - Branch Lines around F 32 1
Derby to Chesterfield G 11 1
Derby to Stoke-on-Trent F 93 2
Derwent Valley - BL to the D 06 7
Devon Narrow Gauge E 09 3
Didcot to Banbury D 02 9
Didcot to Swindon C 84 0
Didcot to Winchester C 13 0
Diss to Norwich G 22 7
Dorset & Somerset NG D 76 0
Douglas - Laxey - Ramsey E 75 8
Douglas to Peel C 88 8
Douglas to Port Erin C 55 0
Douglas to Ramsey D 39 5
Dover to Ramsgate A 78 9
Drem to Edinburgh G 06 7
Dublin Northwards in 1950s E 31 4
Dunstable - Branch Lines to E 27 7
E
Ealing to Slough C 42 0
Eastbourne to Hastings A 27 7
East Cornwall Mineral Railways D 22 7
East Croydon to Three Bridges A 53 6
Eastern Spain Narrow Gauge E 56 7
East Grinstead - BLs to A 07 9
East Kent Light Railway A 61 1
East London - Branch Lines of C 44 4
East London Line B 80 0
East of Norwich - Branch Lines E 69 7
Effingham Junction - BLs a A 74 1
Ely to Norwich C 90 1
Enfield Town & Palace Gates D 32 6
Epsom to Horsham A 30 7
Eritrean Narrow Gauge E 38 3
Euston to Harrow & Wealdstone C 89 5
Exeter to Barnstaple B 15 2
Exeter to Newton Abbot C 49 9
Exeter to Tavistock B 69 5
Exmouth - Branch Lines to B 00 8
F
Fairford - Branch Line to A 52 9
Falmouth, Helston & St. Ives C 74 1
Fareham to Salisbury A 67 3
Faversham to Dover B 05 3
Felixstowe & Aldeburgh - BL to D 20 3
Fenchurch Street to Barking C 20 8
Festiniog - 50 yrs of enterprise C 83 3
Festiniog 1946-55 E 01 7
Festiniog in the Fifties B 68 8
Festiniog in the Sixties B 91 6
Ffestiniog in Colour 1955-82 F 25 3
Finsbury Park to Alexandra Pal C 02 8
French Metre Gauge Survivors F 88 8
Frome to Bristol B 77 0
G
Gainsborough to Sheffield G 17 3
Galashiels to Edinburgh F 52 9
Gloucester to Bristol D 35 7
Gloucester to Cardiff D 66 1
Gosport - Branch Lines around A 36 9
Greece Narrow Gauge D 72 2
Guildford to Redhill A 63 5
H
Hampshire Narrow Gauge D 36 4
Harrow to Watford D 14 2
Harwich & Hadleigh - BLs to F 02 4
Harz Revisited F 62 8
Hastings to Ashford A 37 6
Hawick to Galashiels F 36 9
Hawkhurst - Branch Line to A 66 6
Hayling - Branch Line to A 12 3
Hay-on-Wye - BL around D 92 0
Haywards Heath to Seaford A 28 4
Hemel Hempstead - BLs to D 88 3
Henley, Windsor & Marlow - BLa C77 2
Hereford to Newport D 54 8
Hertford & Hatfield - BLs a E 58 1
Hertford Loop E 71 0
Hexham to Carlisle D 75 3
Hexham to Hawick F 08 6
Hitchin to Peterborough D 07 4
Holborn Viaduct to Lewisham A 81 9
Horsham - Branch Lines to A 02 4
Hull, Hornsea and Withernsea G 27 2
Huntingdon - Branch Line to A 93 2
I
Ilford to Shenfield C 97 0
Ilfracombe - Branch Line to B 21 3
Ilkeston to Chesterfield G 26 5
Ipswich to Diss F 81 9
Ipswich to Saxmundham C 41 3
Isle of Man Railway Journey F 94 9
Isle of Wight Lines - 50 yrs C 12 3
Italy Narrow Gauge F 17 8
K
Kent Narrow Gauge C 45 1
Kettering to Nottingham F 82-6
Kidderminster to Shrewsbury E 10 9
Kingsbridge - Branch Line to C 98 7
Kings Cross to Potters Bar E 62 8
King's Lynn to Hunstanton F 58 1
Kingston & Hounslow Loops A 83 3
Kingswear - Branch Line to C 17 8
L
Lambourn - Branch Line to C 70 3
Launceston & Princetown - BLs C 19 2
Leek - Branch Line From G 01 2
Leicester to Burton F 85 7
Leicester to Nottingham G 15 9
Lewisham to Dartford A 92 5
Lincoln to Cleethorpes F 56 7
Lincoln to Doncaster G 03 6
Lines around Stamford F 98 7
Lines around Wimbledon B 75 6
Lines North of Stoke G 29 6
Liverpool Street to Chingford D 01 2
Liverpool Street to Ilford C 34 5
Llandeilo to Swansea E 46 8
London Bridge to Addiscombe B 20 6
London Bridge to East Croydon A 58 1
Longmoor - Branch Lines to A 41 3
Looe - Branch Line to C 22 2
Loughborough to Ilkeston G 24 1
Loughborough to Nottingham F 68 0
Lowestoft - BLs around E 40 6
Ludlow to Hereford E 14 7
Lydney - Branch Lines around E 26 0
Lyme Regis - Branch Line to A 45 1
Lynton - Branch Line to B 04 6
M
Machynlleth to Barmouth E 54 3
Maesteg and Tondu Lines F 06 2
Majorca & Corsica Narrow Gauge F 41 3
Mansfield to Doncaster G 23 4
March - Branch Lines around B 09 1
Market Drayton - BLs around F 67 3
Market Harborough to Newark F 86 4
Marylebone to Rickmansworth D 49 4
Melton Constable to Yarmouth Bch E031
Midhurst - Branch Lines of E 78 9
Midhurst - Branch Lines to F 00 0
Minehead - Branch Line to A 80 2
Mitcham Junction Lines B 01 5
Monmouth - Branch Lines to E 20 8
Monmouthshire Eastern Valleys D 71 5
Moretonhampstead - BL to C 27 7
Moreton-in-Marsh to Worcester D 26 5
Morpeth to Bellingham F 87 1
Mountain Ash to Neath D 80 7
N
Newark to Doncaster F 78 9
Newbury to Westbury C 66 6
Newcastle to Alnmouth G 36 4
Newcastle to Hexham D 69 2
New Mills to Sheffield G 44 9
Newport (IOW) - Branch Lines to A 26 0
Newquay - Branch Lines to C 71 0
Newton Abbot to Plymouth C 60 4
Newtown to Aberystwyth E 41 3
Northampton to Peterborough F 92 5
North East German NG D 44 9
Northern Alpine Narrow Gauge F 37 6
Northern France Narrow Gauge C 75 8
Northern Spain Narrow Gauge E 83 3
North London Line B 94 7
North of Birmingham F 55 0
North of Grimsby - Branch Lines G 09 8
North Woolwich - BLs around C 65 9
Nottingham to Boston F 70 3
Nottingham twd Kirkby-in-Ashfield G 38 8
Nottingham to Lincoln F 43 7
Nuneaton to Loughborough G 08 1
O
Ongar - Branch Line to E 05 5
Orpington to Tonbridge B 03 9
Oswestry - Branch Lines around E 60 4
Oswestry to Whitchurch E 81 9
Oxford to Bletchley D 57 9
Oxford to Moreton-in-Marsh D 15 9
P
Paddington to Ealing C 37 6
Paddington to Princes Risborough C819
Padstow - Branch Line to B 54 1
Peebles Loop G 19 7
Pembroke and Cardigan - BLs to F 29 1
Peterborough to Kings Lynn E 32 1
Peterborough to Lincoln F 89 5
Peterborough to Newark F 72 7
Plymouth - BLs around B 98 5
Plymouth to St. Austell C 63 5
Pontypool to Mountain Ash D 65 4
Pontypridd to Merthyr F 14 7
Pontypridd to Port Talbot E 86 4
Porthmadog 1954-94 - BLa B 31 2
Portmadoc 1923-46 - BLa B 13 8
Portsmouth to Southampton A 31 4
Portugal Narrow Gauge E 67 3
Potters Bar to Cambridge D 70 8
Preston to Blackpool G 16 6
Princes Risborough - BL to D 05 0
Princes Risborough to Banbury C 85 7
R
Railways to Victory C 16 1
Reading to Basingstoke B 27 5
Reading to Didcot C 79 6
Reading to Guildford A 47 5
Redhill to Ashford A 73 4
Return to Blaenau 1970-82 C 64 2
Rhyl to Bangor F 15 4
Rhymney & New Tredegar Lines E 48 2
Rickmansworth to Aylesbury D 61 6
Romania & Bulgaria NG E 23 9
Romneyrail C 32 1
Ross-on-Wye - BLs around E 30 7
Ruabon to Barmouth E 84 0
Rugby to Birmingham E 37 6
Rugby to Loughborough F 12 3
Rugby to Stafford F 07 9
Rugeley to Stoke-on-Trent F 90 1
Ryde to Ventnor A 19 2
S
Salisbury to Westbury B 39 8
Salisbury to Yeovil B 06 0
Sardinia and Sicily Narrow Gauge F 50 5
Saxmundham to Yarmouth C 69 7
Saxony & Baltic Germany Revisited F 71 0
Saxony Narrow Gauge D 47 0
Scunthorpe to Doncaster G 34 0
Seaton & Sidmouth - BLs to A 95 6
Selsey - Branch Line to A 04 8
Sheerness - Branch Line to B 16 2
Sheffield towards Manchester G 18 0
Shenfield to Ipswich E 96 3
Shrewsbury - Branch Line to A 86 4
Shrewsbury to Chester E 70 3
Shrewsbury to Crewe F 48 2
Shrewsbury to Ludlow E 21 5
Shrewsbury to Newtown E 29 1
Sirhowy Valley Line E 12 3
Sittingbourne to Ramsgate A 90 1
Skegness & Mablethorpe - BL to F 84 0
Slough to Newbury C 56 7
South African Two-foot gauge E 51 2
Southampton to Bournemouth A 42 0
Southend & Southminster BLs E 76 5
Southern Alpine Narrow Gauge F 22 2
Southern France Narrow Gauge C 47 5
South London Line B 46 6
South Lynn to Norwich City F 03 1
Southwold - Branch Line to A 15 4
Spalding - Branch Lines around E
Spalding to Grimsby F 65 9 6
Stafford to Chester F 34 5
Stafford to Wellington F 59 8
St Albans to Bedford D 08 1
St. Austell to Penzance C 67 3
St. Boswell to Berwick F 44 4
Steaming Through Isle of Wight A
Stourbridge to Wolverhampton E
St. Pancras to Barking D 68 5
St. Pancras to Folkestone E 88 8
St. Pancras to St. Albans C 78 9
Stratford to Cheshunt F 53 6
Stratford-u-Avon to Birmingham
Stratford-u-Avon to Cheltenham C
Sudbury - Branch Lines to F 19 2
Surrey Narrow Gauge C 87 1
Sussex Narrow Gauge C 68 0
Swaffham - Branch Lines around
Swanage to 1999 - BL to A 33 8
Swanley to Ashford B 45 9
Swansea - Branch Lines around F
Swansea to Carmarthen E 59 8
Swindon to Bristol C 96 3
Swindon to Gloucester D 46 3
Swindon to Newport D 30 2
Swiss Narrow Gauge C 94 9
T
Talyllyn 60 E 98 7
Tamworth to Derby F 76 5
Taunton to Barnstaple B 60 2
Taunton to Exeter C 82 6
Taunton to Minehead F 39 0
Tavistock to Plymouth B 88 6
Tenterden - Branch Line to A 21 5
Three Bridges to Brighton A 35 2
Tilbury Loop C 86 4
Tiverton - BLs around C 62 8
Tivetshall to Beccles D 41 8
Tonbridge to Hastings A 44 4
Torrington - Branch Lines to B 37
Tourist Railways of France G 04 3
Towcester - BLs around E 39 0
Tunbridge Wells BLs A 32 1
U
Upwell - Branch Line to B 64 0
Uttoxeter to Macclesfield G 05 0
Uttoxetor to Buxton G 33 3
V
Victoria to Bromley South A 98 7
Victoria to East Croydon A 40 6
Vivarais Revisited E 08 6
W
Walsall Routes F 45 1
Wantage - Branch Line to D 25 8
Wareham to Swanage 50 yrs D 0
Waterloo to Windsor A 54 3
Waterloo to Woking A 38 3
Watford to Leighton Buzzard D 45
Wellingborough to Leicester F 73
Welshpool to Llanfair E 49 9
Wenford Bridge to Fowey C 09 3
Westbury to Bath B 55 8
Westbury to Taunton C 76 5
West Cornwall Mineral Rlys D 48
West Croydon to Epsom B 08 4
West German Narrow Gauge D 9
West London - BLs of C 50 5
West London Line B 84 8
West Wiltshire - BLs of D 12 8
Weymouth - BLs A 65 9
Willesden Jn to Richmond B 71 8
Wimbledon to Beckenham C 58 1
Wimbledon to Epsom B 62 6
Wimborne - BLs around A 97 0
Wirksworth - Branch Lines to G 1
Wisbech - BLs around C 01 7
Witham & Kelvedon - BLs a E 82
Woking to Alton A 59 8
Woking to Portsmouth A 25 3
Woking to Southampton A 55 0
Wolverhampton to Shrewsbury E
Wolverhampton to Stafford F 79 6
Worcester to Birmingham D 97 5
Worcester to Hereford D 38 8
Worthing to Chichester A 06 2
Wrexham to New Brighton F 47 5
Wroxham - BLs around F 31 4
Y
Yeovil - 50 yrs change C 38 3
Yeovil to Dorchester A 76 5
Yeovil to Exeter A 91 8
York to Scarborough F 23 9